My HUMMINGBIRD

JJ CARLSON

LUCIDBOOKS

For my brother and sister who also lost a mom and for my dad who lost his soulmate

Table of Contents

One	1
Two	17
Three	24
Four	33
Five	43
Six	63
Seven	68
Eight	83
Nine	90
Ten	104
Eleven	116
Twelve	126
Thirteen	135
Fourteen	138
Fifteen	142
Sixteen	150
Seventeen	157
Eighteen	166
Nineteen	172
Twenty	184

ONE

For the first time in my life, I gagged when I took a bite of my once delicious banana and cinnamon oatmeal. It was the porridge I made every morning and sometimes if I needed a treat, I'd add chocolate chips. But today, it tasted disgusting because today Mom was in surgery. Nothing seemed right.

Mom's body was probably being cut open as I sat there. The image of doctors with gloves and tools in their hands rattled me. I shook my head to clear my thoughts. Mom was going to be okay. The procedure would take away the cancerous tumors, and all would be well again. I just had to wait.

On the next scoop, I wanted to flick the mush at the wall and watch it splat. Before I could do so, I heard a door creak open at the end of the hallway. My sister was up. I peered down the hallway listening to her next move. I felt like I was a cheetah ready to launch after its prey.

My sister took a step out of the doorway, and I raced toward her, abandoning my oatmeal. My brunette hair flopped down my back; the hardwood floor creaked under me.

"Good morning, my beautiful sister!" I rejoiced, my blue eyes bright with gratitude and excitement. I had company. I didn't have to eat my gross oatmeal alone, and I didn't have to think about the hospital.

I am a highly excitable person, and my five-foot-five stature didn't restrict my ability to send waves of good energy. My happiness was similar to that of a child's even though I was twenty-two years old. It was mainly due to my faith.

She looked at me groggy-eyed, still very much asleep. Her blonde hair was tied up in a messy ponytail, and her red silky pajamas, adorned with pink hearts, were rumpled all over. It seemed like she had waged a battle with her covers.

"Do you want to go on a run together this morning?" I asked, yearning for her to say yes.

"Sure." She rubbed her eyes with her fists. "What time?"

"In an hour?" I inquired, attempting to temper my enthusiasm. I knew that if I sounded too eager while she was still groggy, she would become irritated. I couldn't afford to upset her, especially on a day like today, which was already challenging for both of us.

"Okay, let's go to the creek trail," she suggested. The creek trail was simply a bike path along a depleted creek. San Jose didn't have much water to offer.

"Sounds good!" I enveloped her in a tight embrace, wrapping my arms around her rumbled pajamas. With a firm squeeze, I released all my pent-up energy. My hugs were a force of nature. After all these years, she had resigned herself to the fact that I would hug her whether she wanted me to or not. That was just the way it was.

I sauntered back to my bowl of oats at the kitchen table. It seemed more feasible to eat. At least something good was happening today. I was going to run with Mara.

Mara and I are twins, inseparable since birth. We'd often refer to ourselves as "womb mates" to others. She was more than a sister; she was my built-in best friend. However, we chose to attend different colleges, which made us become more independent. When we returned home, we were more thankful for the time we spent together.

Martha was her full name. We called her Mara for short. I thought of Martha from the Bible who consistently played the role of the helper, serving Jesus through physical tasks.

My name didn't grace the pages of the Bible, yet I found solace in it. Jem. Simple to say, easy to recall. Upon researching its meaning, I discovered it signifies "dove." It's an image of peace, a quality I had yet to redeem. Ironically, peace seemed elusive, particularly on a day like today when everything seemed to be shifting for the worse.

"Jem?" Mara's voice echoed from the bathroom, "did Dad remember to buy bananas?" I could anticipate her thoughts. She wanted a banana for her oatmeal. Glancing at my own banana already melting into my oats, I considered offering her mine.

I quickly checked the counter and saw there were three bananas to spare, so I called back to her, "There are bananas!"

Micah entered the kitchen and grabbed the bundle of bananas. "I think I am going to have all these bananas for breakfast." He gave me a devious glance.

"No, stop it!" I bantered back knowing he was only messing around. Micah set the bananas down and opened the fridge.

"Do we have any leftovers?" he asked. I couldn't even remember what we ate last night.

"Uh, I don't know." I scratched my head. How could I forget something so simple? My mind wasn't working right.

Micah was thin and lanky. He was six foot four with muscles that were defined even though he rarely worked out. He barely ever ate breakfast and if he did, it was always leftovers. He was the only person I knew who ate chicken and rice for breakfast. He did this because it was already made, so he didn't have to do anything but grab a fork.

"Ah, a half a piece of chicken." He pulled out the Tupperware, relieved to have something to eat. "I am going to make a sandwich."

Within thirty minutes, Mara had finished eating her bowl of oatmeal and was washing her face when I interrupted her.

"What are you wearing?" I asked, curious to see if I could coordinate with her. I still found it endearing to match her, reminiscent of the days when twins were expected to dress alike.

"Whatever I come across," she replied nonchalantly, without even glancing at me. Her tone left no room for negotiation. It was evident she had no intention of wearing coordinated outfits.

"Uh, okay." I walked back to my room and changed into my gray Nike shirt, black spandex, and gray speckled Nike shoes. A perfect outfit match. Not like it mattered, but it still made me feel good.

Twenty minutes later, we were at the creek trail and setting our watches to get our GPS. Mara ended up wearing her pink zigzag spandex and bright red shirt. Her outfit did not match whatsoever but I decided not to mention it.

I watched her do exactly ten leg swings on each leg as she grabbed onto the sign pole. This was a common warm up move for runners. I, on the other hand, was swinging my arms in big helicopter circles hoping it would pump me up. My body didn't feel like running. But running was what I needed, mainly for my mind.

"Are you ready?" Mara had a confused look on her face. I knew I looked like a total dork waving my arms around, but oddly enough, I felt a little better.

"Almost!" I began doing some jumping jacks to wake up my whole body.

Mara turned away from me and started doing lunges with her lovely long legs. I watched her ponytail bob as she moved. Even in a ponytail, her blonde hair reached halfway down her back. Mara was so gorgeous she could be a model.

Mara was very ambitious. She would always go the extra mile on everything. Two years ago, she hated running, but now she was on the track team at her school and running with me. Education was no different. She had more class credit and internships than I could count, with a job already lined up after college.

My ponytail was way shorter than hers, and my hair was light brown with blonde ends. I had bleached the ends in order to look edgy and fearless, but I didn't quite feel that today. Today was going to be a difficult day. Mom was currently in surgery. As much as we both wanted to control our mom's health, we couldn't. So, we coped by running.

Both our watches beeped almost simultaneously. We were connected to GPS in order to track our miles. Mara gave me a nod, and we were off along the dried-up creek.

After covering two miles, we finally spoke.

"I'm exhausted. Are you feeling tired?" I gasped for breath; our pace was a brisk six minutes per mile.

"I'm alright, but we can take it slower," Mara responded calmly with no indication of fatigue. "How far do you want to go?"

"You decide," I replied, struggling to catch my breath. She showed no sign of slowing down.

"Let's aim for six," she suggested. Of course, she chose six—her favorite number. *Oh dear, six miles ahead. This would be quite the endurance test.* Usually, I was good with six, but my emotions were getting in the mix. *Was it dread? Was it fear?*

"How are you feeling about seeing Mom today?" Roughly twelve more hours until Mom would be discharged from the ICU and ready for visitors.

There was no answer. I turned my head sideways and observed Mara. She had her gaze fixed forward with a straight face. We continued running in silence.

Mara had a knack for being reserved when she chose to be. She approached challenging situations by mulling them over internally before articulating her thoughts.

It reminded me of Jesus's mother, Mary. The Bible said that Mary pondered things in her heart. *Is that what my sister was doing now? Pondering things in her heart?* I envisioned Mary contemplating her life, quietly sifting through her thoughts in prayer.

"We have to be strong," she whispered, her voice catching with emotion, "strong for Mom."

We ran a few steps in silence. I blinked rapidly, fighting back tears, refocusing on the gravity of our situation.

"You're right," I affirmed. "We need to be strong, together." We locked our eyes, silently communicating our shared determination. I could see the glistening of tears in her eyes, just as I'm sure she could see mine.

* * *

Before anyone knew it, I had known there was something wrong with Mom. Early on in the summer, her stomach had a large bulge to it that I had never seen before.

Mom was beautiful. She had brown wavy hair that went to her shoulders with bangs that helped round out her oval face. Her eyes were ocean blue, and her smile was big so that when she entered a room, she could really brighten it up.

Mom was tall, five feet eight, and naturally thin, which was why it was so upsetting to see her stomach appear so irregular. It didn't make sense.

When I confronted her about my worry, she was in denial. She dismissed it and said it was her abs swelling from her Pilates class.

But as time went on, her belly grew. It was strange to me that my mom could obtain a stomach this round. She had a fast metabolism, ate a well-rounded diet, and I would say she'd stay healthy all her life. I was a D1 athlete running for the Oregon State Track team. I knew what Pilates did to your abs. Pilates makes you slimmer in the mid-section, not larger. It didn't make sense.

Soon, her stomach started growing even larger. My fear escalated. After a month, I confronted her again. I wasn't going to let it slide this time. I remember the moment clearly because I asked to go on a walk with her. We always liked to go on casual walks around the neighborhood. I remember stopping her near the end of our walk—at a random driveway.

"Hey Mom," I blurted, unsure of how she would react to what I was about to say.

"Yes, honey," she replied.

"I, uh, well I don't want to be mean, but you look pregnant, and I know you said it was your abs, but I don't believe it," I said frankly. I stopped and faced her so she would know I was serious.

"No, it's just swollen because of my ab routine," she declared with a slight echo of concern in her voice.

"Mom, you have to face it. Your belly doesn't look natural; it is too perfectly round. Your stomach keeps growing, and I think you should see a doctor. It's not normal. I know it's not normal." I outlined her belly with my finger and gave her a look. Our eyes locked, and there was mutual silence, an understanding, but also fear.

"You HAVE to see a doctor," I demanded. I continued to lock eyes with hers. "Please see a doctor," I pleaded. "Please."

That doctor's appointment sent her to surgery. She had four liters of water in her stomach secreted by a cancerous tumor. Mom tried joking with us by saying that it was like having five bottles of wine inside you. We couldn't find any humor with this news, not when we had to be the ones watching our mom be attacked by cancer.

It was ovarian cancer. First, it started in the ovaries, and then the tumor formed. They had to do surgery to take out as much as they could before it spread further. The doctor said we were lucky we had an outward sign of the cancer or else they wouldn't have found it. I wouldn't call anything about our situation lucky.

I remember thinking, *Is this real? A cancerous tumor secreting water in my mom's abdomen?* I retreated to my bedroom and shifted my body to the side of my bed, knees down on the hardwood floor. I had to clasp my hands in prayer to get them to be still.

I steadied my gaze on the one image of Jesus I had on my nightstand.

"Jesus, I don't know what's going on. I'm shocked. Does she really have cancer?" I paused and waited for a response. There was only silence.

I continued. "I don't want her to have cancer. Please help us stay strong through this." My mouth turned dry, and I didn't know what else to say.

I felt my heart getting weak with worry. I needed strength. We were all going to need strength. "Jesus, please, strength," I muttered before I flung myself on my bed with my face pressed deep into my pillow.

I remembered there was a lot of deep breathing and I looked at my ceiling collaged with Bible verses I had written over the years. I searched for a verse to find inspiration. *"Hope does not disappoint"* (Romans 5:5). I read it again in the hope it would uplift my heart.

"I hope we're going to be okay," I prayed. I turned my head sideways and fixed my eyes on the blank wall to my left. I didn't remember anything after that.

* * *

We embarked to the hospital with my dad and brother in our weathered dark blue Acura that desperately needed a wash. Its cleanliness was the least of our worries. My dad was silent. His blue-gray eyes focused on the road ahead.

Dad and Mom were happily married, which created a happy family dynamic. They met in their thirties at a party met at a party where they were both working in San Luis Obispo. She was a nurse, and he was an accountant. I think Mom was the one who asked Dad to dance. The rest is history as they say.

Our family was very loving. Aside from the sarcastic remarks by Micah or harmless arguments with Mara, we cherished family time because we genuinely enjoyed each other's company. Vacations often included camping, hiking, and other outdoor activities, which not only helped us appreciate life's offerings but also strengthened our family bonds.

Everyone was passionate about sports. We were a soccer family until Mara and I discovered running, which thrilled Dad as it was his passion too. While Mom enjoyed watching sports, she preferred participating in hiking, Pilates, and biking. Micah was the only one who still played soccer.

On the drive to the hospital, everyone was silent. Micah occupied the passenger seat, seemingly at ease with the quietude surrounding us. Micah's perpetual calmness was a trait I admired. In moments like these, when I struggled to find my own inner peace, his presence provided a comforting refuge.

Mara, who sat next to me, was staring off into space, so I decided that I should do that too. With clean damp hair clinging to my skin, I rested my head against the window, observing the passing cars in the adjacent lane.

ONE

With Dad's guidance, we found the surgery clinic. After the initial visit, he had already memorized the layout of the unit. He never needed directions.

My dad received a call from the doctor, who assured him that the surgery had been successful, although Mom would require a considerable amount of time to recover. The doctor had skillfully extracted her ovaries and eliminated all visible tumors. Mom's body would need time to adapt to the significant changes after the procedure.

The post-surgery floor was awfully quiet, and I soon realized that healing from surgery required a lot of sleep. When we entered Mom's hospital room, she was lying motionless. The whole scene was so surreal that I blinked repeatedly to confirm its reality.

Aside from her stillness, her appearance was greatly altered. Her body was swollen from head to toe. Her skin was flushed and her body stiff. She was completely vulnerable.

Approaching with a sense of disbelief, I noticed the pinkish puffiness in her face as I tried to find the features that normally made my mom look like my mom. I inspected her round, plump cheeks, which were three sizes larger than normal. Her eyelids were puffy with splotches of magenta and her nose seemed to be the only thing unchanged.

I scanned the rest of her body. Every limb was swollen as if air had been pumped through her like a bounce house. I felt a deep well of empathy for her, prompting me to reach out and grasp the hand not entwined with tubes.

Her hand was limp but warm. I pressed my palm into hers, offering a reassuring squeeze before softly rubbing my thumb back and forth across her skin. I never wanted to let go.

The small motion of rubbing my thumb on her skin made my heart sink. I forced back my quivering lip but was unable to stop the tears from running down my cheeks. I didn't have enough strength to hold them in.

A knock echoed through the room, announcing the arrival of Doctor Raymond. He had a cheerful presence about him, which made me like him instantly. His head was balding with age and his stature was sturdy. I couldn't help but notice his New Balance athletic shoes giving off distinct dad vibes. I wondered if he had children.

"Hello family of Colette," he said. He looked each one of us in the eye while we introduced ourselves in front of our unconscious mother.

"I'm the husband," my dad said as he stepped forward like it was a role call and shook Doctor Raymond's hand.

"I'm Jem," I said, smiling.

"I'm Mara."

"I'm Micah." We waited for what he was going to say next.

Doctor Raymond cleared his throat. "As you can see Colette is responding to the surgery well. She has a lot of inflammation which is vital to the healing process. We were able to take out the spleen easily and now we are making sure her fluid levels stay consistent. She is on a large dose of pain medication so there's no need to worry about anything."

We all stared at him, each making a gesture of recognition. *Did he really say not to worry?* I don't think that was possible.

"I'll let you be alone with her now." Doctor Raymond gently closed the door behind him, but our eyes weren't on him, they were already on mom, our unconscious, bloated, lifeless mom.

Despite the surgery's supposed aid to my mom, there was no evidence of improvement in her outward appearance. She seemed more dead than alive. The only movement came from the faint rise and fall of her chest. I maintained my grip on her hand, unwilling to let go.

As I clasped her hand in silence, I noticed her index finger shift slightly, a subtle indication of her awareness. A tear escaped from my right eye, trailing swiftly down my cheek before settling onto the hospital bed. I squeezed her hand gently, communicating that I felt her.

I heard a hum from Mom's lips, a sure sign of contentment from my hand squeeze. More tears streamed down my face, and I couldn't control them. Tears of agony mixed with tears of hope. Hope that she was going to get better, that what the doctor said was true.

Behind me, I sensed my dad shuffling uncomfortably, unable to bear witnessing Mom so vulnerable. Micah remained lodged in the corner of the room, rendered speechless by Mom's state. As for Mara, I could tell she was silently grappling with the daunting prospect of what lay ahead, her inner turmoil raging.

I knew we all wanted to do something about her situation, to make her better, to make her pain go away but we couldn't. We were powerless. The only thing I could do was hold her hand so she could know I was there.

A gentle knock interrupted the room, but instead of Doctor Raymond, a blonde nurse entered, her hair hastily pulled into a bun atop her head, compassion radiated from her eyes. Clad in scrubs, she approached, holding a sizable needle filled with clear liquid.

"Hi, I'm Clare. I'm the other nurse that's been taking care of your mom. She is absolutely a wonderful woman. Before surgery, she had us all laughing." The statement made me loosen up a bit, knowing Mom was in a good mood hours before her surgery.

Clare continued, "I'm here to give your mom some pain medication. The needle hurts a little but then everything will be okay."

We watched as Clare injected the pain medication into Mom's left wrist. Instantly, there was a deep moan that escaped from Mom's inflamed lips. I gave her a squeeze to reassure her I was here.

Like a waterfall, tears escaped down my face aggressively. I couldn't hold them back anymore. *My mom's in pain!* I wanted to scream. *The needle is hurting her! Stop the pain, just stop it!* I pulled my head down and bit my bottom lip to keep me from sobbing and yelling at the nurse.

"Everything is going to be fine; this is going to help her," Clare reassured. I didn't look up. I heard her footsteps slowly back away. "I will be back to check on her in a little while." She left the room, avoiding the heartbreak that appeared on all our faces.

I stood over Mom and used my other hand to stroke her hair. I delicately placed the tips of my fingers on the crown of her forehead and ran my fingers back a couple inches through her hair to where her head met the pillow. Even though her eyes were closed, I gazed at her, and my lips shifted into a slight smile. I hoped that she could sense it.

Mom loved to get her hair stroked. It was a simple pleasure for her. Many times, she would beg me to rub her head and if I resisted, she'd playfully grip my hand and place it on her forehead. I hoped she could feel it now.

I leaned in closer and kissed her on the check.

A faint "I love you" emerged from Mom's lips. I almost jumped with glee. She knew it was me.

"I love you too, Mommy! I love you so, so much!" I squealed. I felt a sense of gratitude as a new set of tears emerged from my eyes. Now, Mara, Micah, my dad, and I were crying, each repeating the words "I love you" in harmony.

That night I propped my elbows on my bed covers and stationed my knees on the hardwood floor. I liked praying like this because the hardwood against my knees kept me awake. I had my dad take out the carpet so I could pretend I was in a wood cabin.

The walls of my room boasted a light brown hue, supporting the wood cabin ambiance. Deep red curtains adorned the window, casting a warm pinkish glow throughout the space. This subtle tint was soothing especially during my afternoon naps.

Above my bed there was a blown-up photo of a tiger's head, looking both majestic and aggressive. Its eyes were emerald in color, which made it mesmerizing to look at. Below the image, I had a painted Bible verse that read, *"This is the day the Lord has made let us rejoice and be glad"* (Psalm 118:24). It was particularly hard to read today since I was feeling quite sad and lacked the inclination to find joy in anything.

My knees were wobbly from the intensity of the hardwood on my kneecaps. I welcomed the pain; I didn't have the energy to fight it. I raised my eyes to an empty spot on my plain brown wall and imagined God in the room with me.

"In the name of the Father and the Son and the Holy Spirit." I prayed and motioned the sign of the cross. In this time of prayer, I would choose to be grateful. "God, thank You for making my mom's surgery go well. I'm glad I got to see her and hold her hand." I imagined her in the hospital bed, unable to move and I shed a tear.

"Thank You that the doctors and nurses are taking care of her." I thought of Clare and the needle, and more tears slid down my cheek. "But God, I'm scared. She looks so bad. I'm scared that she's in pain."

I couldn't bear the thought of Mom suffering, of her battling cancer. Mom was the one who comforted me. *How could I comfort her?* Overwhelmed by emotions, I collapsed forward, surrendering to complete exhaustion. My body lay sprawled on the floor, face buried in tears.

As the tears subsided, I took a deep breath and composed myself. Returning to a prayerful position, my knees ached from the physical strain. My eyes failed to open.

"God, please embrace me tonight. I need Your strength. Please watch over my family. They're hurting too. And, dear God, please guide my mom to recovery. Amen." I crawled under the covers and felt a wave of longing, reminiscent of childhood nights when all I craved was for my mom to kiss me goodnight.

TWO

Sleep usually never comes when you need it the most. I was running low on sleep, but my dad seemed to have had none.

"Morning, Dad," I said upon entering the kitchen. In comparison to yesterday, this day seemed doable. I wanted to make sure he thought so too. Dad didn't look up. He appeared a little too focused on his last bite of cereal.

"Morning," he answered, still avoiding eye contact.

I know he was avoiding my gaze to hide the residue of his tears. He didn't want me to see the deep eye bags, the evidence of his fatigue and restlessness. He was trying to hide his pain.

My dad was tall like Micah, standing just an inch below him. He had dark brown hair that was transitioning into dark gray, which was receding at a slow but noticeable rate. He kept in shape by walking or biking, less demanding activities than running.

Dad used to run but the scoliosis in his back worsened, and he had to give it up. I think he relived his running days when he watched Mara and I run. He loved watching us run.

Dad's number one priority was making sure our family was having fun and that we felt cared for. Mom's illness hit us all hard, but I couldn't imagine the fear he had for her and our family tucked away in his heart.

I leaned over to my dad who was still sitting at the kitchen table and gave him a hug. I refrained from asking how he was, so he didn't have to tell me. No one likes telling people they're sad. He didn't ask me how I was either.

I marched into the kitchen to grab a glass of water because my mouth was parched. Just as I filled my cup, he stood up.

"I'm going to the hospital. We'll take turns. I'll be back in a couple hours." He took his empty cereal bowl and placed it by the sink. Then he was out the door before I could say anything else.

I sighed. I knew I was going to be alone for the rest of the morning. I knew Micah and Mara were going to sleep for a while. At two in the morning, I saw the light on in Mara's room when I went to the bathroom. There was no way she would wake up early.

Micah would sleep in late no matter what state of mind he was in. Though, whatever was on Micah's mind was rarely said. He kept his emotions to himself, just like my dad. It was Mara who I needed to confide in.

Since both my siblings were sleeping in, I was next in line for my visit with Mom. This gave me hope. Maybe I could cheer her up. That was going to be my goal. I was going to put on my happy girl pants and bring her some encouragement.

Once my dad returned, he dropped the keys in my hands, and I was off. I had nothing on me but my phone, wallet, and

Rosary. On the way to the hospital, I put on the Christian station and tried to relax. The songs were upbeat and cheesy, but it gave me a sense of lighthearted innocence, something that easily gets lost when you become an adult.

After fifteen minutes, I pulled up in the visitors parking space at Valley Medical Center. I never felt like we were in a valley because San Jose was such a big city. It's easy to forget about the mountains when you are worrying about traffic all the time.

Just like most hospitals, this one was huge. Dad said Mom had changed rooms overnight. He gave me verbal directions, but when I stepped through the automatic doors, I forgot it all. I decided to just keep walking straight until I could find someone to help me.

"Hi, are you looking for someone?" a bubbly blonde nurse asked me. She was different from the one yesterday; she had curly hair and a sturdy figure. Her cheeks were plump in the right way with a slight pink tint. She read my confused expression. Mara said I wore my heart on my sleeve, which was a nice way of saying that I couldn't mask my emotions. I was an open book.

"Yeah, I'm looking for my mom, Colette. She had surgery, and they moved her to a new room." I realized that my answer was vague. I instantly felt dumb.

"Oh . . . Colette! What a lovely and funny mother you have! She's on the third floor in room 30A." I couldn't believe that of all the patients she knew my mom.

"Thank you so much!" I grinned and strutted my way to the stairs leaving the hefty blonde nurse to continue her rounds. I giggled to myself: *Of course, Mom had made friends with the whole hospital!*

Mom was a friend to everyone. With her outgoing spirit, she could talk to anyone anytime and anywhere. She could chat someone up in the parking lot, by the sinks in the bathroom, even in the tampon section of Walmart. The minute she talked to someone, she made them feel known, like a friend. No hospital bed confinement could stop her.

I failed to get the name of the lovely blonde nurse but as soon as I explained the encounter, Mom knew exactly who she was.

"Oh . . . Lucy! She's so nice! She likes green tea like me. Though I can't drink caffeine right now." Her voice sounded almost normal, and she was sitting upright. There was color in her face again.

"They are taking good care of me here." She tapped the bed to signal me to come closer.

As she smiled, I fully registered that she was making tremendous progress. The puffiness in her cheeks had decreased, and I could see the crinkles in her cheek. Her body was less stiff and smaller. I looked at her fingers. They were less swollen. I immediately grabbed one of her hands to give it a tight squeeze. She felt human again.

I looked back up at her face and saw her beautiful pink lips again. It was evident that her body was rebounding from the surgery. My heart leaped with hope. *There was hope.*

"Mommy!" I exclaimed like a five-year-old finding her doll before bedtime. "I love you so much!" I quickly pulled my chest toward her until I remembered that she was fragile, so I slowed down and gracefully touched my heart to hers. I placed my palms on the back of the bed to keep most of my weight off her. She needed this hug, but I felt like I needed it more.

As one who finds nature a healing remedy, I thought it would be a good idea to get some fresh air. Being inside all day can feel stuffy.

"How about we see the sunshine?!" I happily asked. The suggestion left my mouth right before my brain said *she's in a hospital bed, silly!*

The blonde nurse whose name I now knew was Lucy, passed our room as my suggestion lingered in midair. Lucy was checking to see if I had made it to my mom. I liked her name. It reminded me of Saint Lucy who was the patron saint of those who were blind. She stopped when she heard me and popped her head into the open room.

"Oh, honey!" she exclaimed, "that's a great idea. I can go grab a wheelchair right now and set you two up." Lucy scampered away in search of one.

A smile spread across my mother's face.

"I'd love some fresh air," she mused. "I'm getting tired of sitting inside. I'm also getting tired of all these IVs." She shifted in her bed, which I could imagine was getting uncomfortable. I was excited to have her get some California vitamin D and some time away from the confines of the bed.

In the blink of an eye, Lucy rolled the wheelchair over to our room. She looked more excited than mom. For a moment I imagined Saint Lucy, healing the blind. This Lucy was like Saint Lucy in her own way. We were blind from the sunshine, but not for long.

"Okay, Colette, before I help you into the wheelchair, I am going to disconnect you from the machine." Mom and I both nodded in acknowledgement. Lucy had to disconnect about five

IVs in order to set her free from the bed.

Unlatching the tubes was the easy thing. The hard thing was transferring Mom to the wheelchair. It took both our best efforts to slide my mom to the left side of the bed, lift her up, and gently settle her in the chair. Even though she was thinner than yesterday, she still had a lot of water weight.

When we got her situated, I rolled Mom to the hospital courtyard. There was nobody else out there, and I was relieved. I wanted private time with her.

I propped Mom in a half-sun and half-shade location while I took a seat in full sun. It was beautiful outside, and we both took a deep breath in unison and smiled. A minute later, she wasn't smiling anymore. Her reality had set in.

"Jem, look at me. I can't believe it," she cried. "I have cancer. I'm too young to have cancer. This isn't supposed to happen." My eyes softened and I felt a deep wave of sympathy for her. I reached out and touched her hand.

"Will I ever have a normal life again?" She squeezed my hand, as if she was begging me to give me back her life. But I wasn't in charge of that. *Was it God? Or was it under nature's control?*

Her outburst of hopelessness was devastating. I quickly tried to come up with something that would cheer her up. I needed to reassure her. I needed to encourage her. That's what I came to do. *What would she say to me?*

"Mom," I started, "of course you'll have your normal life back again. You'll recover in no time, and you'll be stronger and—"

"How do you know?!" she interrupted, crying even louder. "How do you know I'll get better and do the things I was doing and go on trips and go hiking and everything?!" She let go of my hand to wipe the tears away. "I don't want to die!" she shrieked, and it rattled me to the core.

I didn't want her to die either. It didn't even cross my mind that she was going to die. She went to the doctors. She got surgery. She will be healed. That was that.

I had never seen Mom in this state of distress. Mara and I promised each other that we'd be strong for Mom. I had to be strong.

"Mom don't say that. It's going to be okay." I stood up and gave her a side hug over the wheelchair and kissed the top of her head. Then I stood next to her in silence and rubbed her head. With my other hand I squeezed my Rosary beads and sent up a prayer. We stayed there, until her tears stopped.

When I got home, I was drained. There was nothing I wanted to do but nap. So, I went into my room and let the pink tint of my curtains soothe me to sleep. I didn't think my mom's life was meant to be over. She had so much of her life to live. This was just a road bump or pothole or maybe a full-on crash. But it wasn't over. Before I dozed off, I prayed silently that God would agree with me.

THREE

A week went by, and Mom was finally stable enough to be released from the hospital. Micah, Mara, and I paced with anticipation for her arrival. Mom was coming home. Finally. Mom and home never felt so perfect in a sentence before.

After what seemed like hours of waiting, I heard Dad's gentle voice.

"Nice and easy, Colette."

I scrambled off the couch and opened the door as Micah and Mara approached behind me. My jaw dropped to my shoulder. She was barely standing. I thought a week in the hospital meant she had the ability to move normally. Boy was I wrong.

Before I could blink, Mara was holding Mom's right side while Dad stood opposite, holding her left. Mom's hands were clutching onto an unfamiliar walker. My jaw stayed dropped. My feet wouldn't move.

Micah held the front door open, giving space for Dad and Mara to spot Mom as she took the one cement step up the pathway.

"It's okay, Colette, we got you." I could tell Dad's tender voice calmed her. Mara grabbed Mom's right leg and placed it on top of the step. Together, Mara and Dad lifted her up to the next level as she held tight to the walker that was before her.

The sight of my mother's figure was disorienting to say the least. Her normally slim arms and chest looked even smaller in comparison to her waist-down figure. From her hips to her toes, she was very enlarged. The excess fluid from the surgery was still circulating in her lower body. The inflammation caused so much inflation that her lower body looked stuffed with feathers.

Once Mom wobbled in the doorway with the continuous help from my dad and sister, they sat her down on her favorite recliner in the room with the windows. We called this room the front room because well, it was the room in the front of the house.

As Mom sat, Mara made a point to prop up her giant legs. Mom made a point to tell us how giant her legs were.

"I know I look funny," she said looking at us. "My legs are huge!" We all laughed while Dad left the room. He wasn't in the mood for laughter.

I was happy to see that Mom's personality was back and that her hopeless state was nowhere to be found.

Mom was happy too, even though her body wasn't. I peered down at her large legs that were propped up by the brown recliner we bought from Costco. I started poking at her cushion-looking legs with my finger.

"I can't believe they got that big," I said, still shocked, unbelieving that my mom's legs were capable of growing.

"It's sorta like blubber," Micah said with a grin. It did look very blubbery. I wondered what was going on inside. We all laughed again, standing in a circle around Mom's chair. It felt good to laugh.

"I know they're huge!" Mom declared again with a lighthearted annoyance. "The swelling is supposed to go down soon, and these stockings will help." She pulled up her pajama bottoms, which were skintight, and showed us her stockings.

They seemed like normal fancy tan stockings that a lady would wear to the orchestra on a Saturday night in the city. However, if you looked closer, you could see the stockings were clutching her thighs as if their goal was to turn her legs purple. It didn't look very comfortable.

"They are tight, but I can't really feel it. They're supposed to help with the swelling," she explained. "I hope this puffiness goes away soon—I look like an Oompa Loompa!" We all laughed again. Mom's attitude was back, and I sure liked this version better.

"Now, I need to go to the bathroom." She rolled onto her right side and clutched the chair to get up.

Mara looked afraid and touched her elbow. "Do you need help, Mom?"

"No, honey. I want to do it myself." We nervously watched Mom waddle into the hallway.

"Nice waddle, Mom!" I cheered, making us all laugh again. I was trying to keep the lighthearted spirit alive.

Mom yelled from the bathroom, and the laughter stopped. "Help! I need help!" We could hear her voice echo through the hallway.

Mara raced down the hallway, and I could hear her speaking with a warm tone as if she was a nurse. Then we heard sounds of barfing, and I covered my ears.

There was no more laughter after that.

* * *

As much as we didn't like the change, we had to adjust the best we could. Dad started working from home on the only computer in the house, which was in the kitchen nook. I got a nice view of him sifting through his Excel spreadsheets as I shoveled through my oatmeal. A couple days of seeing what accounting was like was enough for me to feel sorry for all accountants.

I was up at seven most days because the sun shined through my red drapes kissing me awake. It was early summer, but instead of the anticipation of camping, day trips, and ice cream, there was a feeling of dread that Mom would barf up her breakfast.

It was mid-June, so none of us kids were in school. This was probably the highlight of the whole situation. We were all home, and we all could help.

Almost instantly, Mara took over as Mom's primary caregiver. It was not even a question that she could do the job better than any of us. Her innate care and selflessness exceeded that of anyone I knew. Her motherlike nature was superior to her intense competitive drive. I was impressed that she held both generosity and ambition in one identity.

In between caring for mom, Mara would join me on my seven-mile runs and then spend hours accomplishing her online accounting classes. I was surprised she didn't drop the class after seeing Dad on his never-ending spreadsheets. She decided to stick with a major in accounting and finance.

The thing about Mara was that she never quit. She was just like Martha in the Bible, never quitting until the job is done, until the mess is cleaned, until the duty is finished. It was rare when I would find her sitting down in one place. The most she'd sit was when she was reading a book and even then, she was accomplishing something because she was keeping Mom company on the couch.

As Dad's accounting job came to an end, his therapy job began. Through the closed door to their bedroom, I could hear Dad listening to Mom purging all her frustration and pain from the day, both mentally and physically sapped. Dad, as much as he wanted a break, never really had one.

Unlike Dad who had a schedule, Micah didn't. He was out of college and was currently job searching. With an engineering degree, he had a right to be picky. He was very choosy about his next job, which was good for Mom because he was always home, and he probably would be home for quite some time.

Micah lived on the opposite side of the house, in the garage to be exact. The walls were newly insulated, and Dad had insisted he have a window, so it wouldn't be a dungeon. Sometimes, when I took out the trash from the side yard, I'd peer in his window and wave hello. He was usually on his computer researching jobs or investigating the stock market.

Micah was smart, and he was well-rounded on many topics. He liked to debate and discuss random topics as if we were old men playing a game of pool. I enjoyed these discussions because they allowed me to learn something new without having to read any articles.

As for me, I defaulted as the substitute mom. I cooked the meals, and I cleaned the house whenever it was needed. I smiled wide and encouraged Mom that things would get better and that everything was going to be okay. Mom was the glue that held us together with her service and her support. Now was my time to do that for her and the rest of the family.

After two weeks, I felt myself becoming frustrated that Mom wasn't healing quick enough. I didn't understand why she wouldn't eat a proper meal or why she wouldn't go on a walk with me. I was determined to get her to do both because that was what healthy people did, and I needed Mom to be healthy.

I crept into the room with the big windows and put on my big Jem smile and engaged my big Jem energy.

"Hey, Mom!" I sat down next to her, my butt on the floor as she sprawled out on the couch. I had been examining her legs and saw that the swelling had gone. Her body had become frail, and she needed to gain some weight. She had not yet returned to a regular eating routine or exercise regimen and was primarily confined to bed rest.

The couch became Mom's reserved spot in the house along with the Costco recliner next to it. It was a dark olive color which I found ugly. However, this couch had the most cushiony pillows, so soft that your butt would immediately find comfort the moment you sat in it.

"Hey, honey. I was just looking at my Spotify, and I realized I can click on any song and find a radio station that matches it." Her face showed nothing but delight.

"Nice! Now, you'll be able to browse more music." Music was a good distraction in her immobile state. She was spending much of her days indoors. "How about we take a walk outside? We can listen to the music of the birds." I flashed her a hopeful smile.

"Jem, I'm feeling very tired. Why don't we go tomorrow?" I knew that we wouldn't go tomorrow if we didn't go today. I had to drag her out.

"Mom, I know you're tired, but we can take a really short walk. I know you will feel better after. Fresh air always heals the soul. How about we walk past five houses? Only five and then we walk back," I assured her. "I'll be with you, and we can go as slow as you want." I tried to make it sound like I was giving her a deal.

She hesitated a moment before she answered. "Okay, five houses." She gave me a smirk signaling that I had won. I leaped to my feet and raced to grab her Birkenstocks.

I slid the sandals over her thick fuzzy socks, the only shoes that would fit her still inflamed feet. I held her elbow as support, and we were hobbling out the door before she could change her mind.

When we got down the driveway, Mom's eyes lit up. It was a usual sunny afternoon in California; the blue sky was beaming overhead. I could see Mom's chest rise and fall. It was her first breath of fresh air in days. We tottered down the street with her weak body next to mine.

We assessed the front lawns and architecture of each house we walked past. With the slow-motion speed we were going in, it was easy to see the small details of each neighbor's property. I admired the bright yellow door of a newly painted house. It was the color of a highlighter. I wasn't sure if I loved it or hated it. Maybe I hated it so much I loved it, just like the green couch.

A pigeon soared above us, releasing its poop onto the sidewalk a foot in front of us. The resulting splatter echoed loudly, eliciting laughter from Mom and me. Had we been walking any faster, we might not have been so lucky.

"Glad we weren't in the splash zone," Mom reported. We were hesitant to continue, and we were at the fifth house just like I'd promised.

"It was a sign," I declared, and we giggled our way back home. The walk was a win, a small win, but a win, nonetheless. I was going to take it.

* * *

After that day, I decided I was going to be the fun one. I was going to send Mom into a new way of life that made her feel less sick and more her. I wanted to be a light in her life, constantly lifting her up and to distract her when she was feeling down.

In every moment I could find, I'd happily skip to her and ask her how she was. If she was good, I'd chat with her and try to get her to go on a walk. If she wasn't good, I'd do my best to distract her with a random story until Mara came to be her nurse. That was my cue to step out.

When Mom summoned Mara, it meant she required real medical assistance. Mara was the only one who could watch Mom vomit, aid her in her accidents, and undress her fragile and deteriorating body without displaying a hint of sympathy or sadness. Mara maintained a stoic expression throughout these moments. I marveled at her resilience; it was a testament to true strength.

The thought of her dependence frightened me. The fact that she relied on assistance to use the bathroom and to dress herself was unsettling. Fear of her sudden bouts of vomiting, her cries of pain, and her visible suffering filled me with dread. These times of distress were unsettling and, in those times, all I could do was wait until she felt better and pray.

"Thank you so much, Mara," I'd hear Mom say with gratitude. *Thank you, Mara,* I hummed in my head. *What would we do without you?*

FOUR

Each day I continued to wake up determined to find hope as I followed the Bible verse on my ceiling. *"Hope does not disappoint,"* I reassured myself. After breakfast, I'd go on a run with Mara and then check in on Mom. Same routine every day but with new hope each morning.

Weeks were flying by, and my mind often wandered to returning to school and preparing for the cross-country season. I longed for the camaraderie of my teammates, the companionship of my roommate, and the joyous laughter that accompanied it all. Thoughts of going back to school stirred up guilt within me. *Could I really leave Mom like this?*

I felt confined in this house, confined around the sadness of Mom's condition. The situation was disheartening, and I felt suffocated by the overwhelming gloom of it all. I desired to support Mom, but it was becoming incredibly difficult to watch her suffer.

I needed to think of other things besides cancer. There was only one more month of summer left, and I had to make a decision. I could go back to Oregon State, or I could take online classes from home. Both decisions were good in their own way, but I had to decide what would be best.

I shrugged off my thoughts and headed toward the kitchen to see if Mom wanted anything to eat. Mom's body had returned completely to its usual state, devoid of inflammation. However, despite this improvement, her continued lack of appetite was evident in the visible loss of pounds. What little she did manage to consume often ended up being regurgitated. It was hard to watch.

I walked up to Mom who was sitting at the table with a cracker on her plate looking nauseous. I gently patted her back. "It's okay, Mom; just try eating something else," I encouraged. It was crucial to keep trying.

"Do we have any popsicles?" she asked wide-eyed. We hadn't eaten popsicles since I was ten years old. We definitely did not have any in our freezer.

"Are you sure you want a popsicle? What about a smoothie?" I suggested something that I knew we had in the freezer and something more appropriate for breakfast.

"No, I'd really like a popsicle. A cherry one. Or an orange one." Before I could answer, Dad entered the room.

"I'll go to the store right now and get some, hun." Dad leaned over and kissed her on the cheek and turned around quickly to grab his keys.

"Thanks, hun," she called after him. Dad was already out the door. I sat beside her and placed my arm on her shoulder.

"Crackers are boring. I think you need something tasty." I cracked a smile and dished together a bowl of banana chocolate oatmeal and retrieved two spoons.

"Here you go. We can share." I handed her the spoon. "You can get the first bite." I pointed at the chocolate chip that was melted by the microwave. Mom followed suit and scooped the chocolate chunk up with the oatmeal underneath. She took a bite and assessed.

"Wow, this is good!" She hummed, and she had another bite. I pushed the bowl in her direction. "You have it. I can make another one for myself."

We sat together eating chocolate banana oats, and I felt proud of her. I was pleased she was eating, and I was elated that she was eating a normal amount. My oats tasted better than normal because there was the secret ingredient, hope. And I was not disappointed.

Dad came back within twenty minutes and placed the party-size box of popsicles on the kitchen table. I was sure he got the extra-large pack wishing Mom would eat the whole box as a meal. The package had cherry, grape, and orange flavored popsicles. I wondered if the grape was ever going to see the light of day.

The popsicle I grabbed was orange. I unwrapped it and held it out to Mom. Surprisingly, she took it and licked it roughly five times.

"This tastes way better than when I was a kid!" Mom remarked. She had a couple more licks, but then she was full. I smiled and took the rest of the popsicle to the sink so it could melt. Progress. She was making progress.

Later that afternoon, Mom had a checkup with Doctor Raymond. He said Mom had to go to chemotherapy because it was needed to kill the cancer cells that the surgery couldn't take out. Of course, he mentioned that chemotherapy would also kill the healthy cells, but it was the only option to defeat cancer. Reluctantly, Mom agreed. She would do anything to get rid of it.

As we sat down for dinner, which I now consistently cooked, we were all in consensus that Mom was starting chemotherapy this week. I had made chicken, brown rice, and broccoli for the family, which was a healthy combination of protein, carbs, and veggies.

"This meal needs more salt," Micah announced as he was chewing. He sat next to me and made a disgusted face. Feeling underappreciated, I grabbed the saltshaker from the kitchen counter and tossed it at him.

"Well then, you can salt it to your liking. I think the meal is delicious," I sassed back. Mara eyed Micah.

"Can you pass the salt to me next?" Of course, Mara wanted more salt; both her and Micah liked intense flavor. I almost rolled my eyes. I gazed at Dad, and he was happily chomping on his meal. At least he enjoyed it.

The best part of the night was seeing my mom finish her small plate. I was so happy, I wanted to jump up and down and congratulate her, but I forced myself to stay put and silent. I was not going to make her feel like a child. So, I kept the happiness in my heart alive, and I made a mental note to thank God later that night.

Chemotherapy was three times a week for three months. It sounded like a college course. It also seemed pretty intense. It was going to be a very tiring process, but it was the standard procedure for cancer patients.

One afternoon, Mom was reading a booklet about the side effects of chemo. It was a thick four-hundred-page book. I glanced over her shoulder, and I could see medical terminology. I swooped the packet out of her hand.

"Mom! You should not be reading this! Have you heard of the placebo effect? If you read this stuff, your body is going to follow it." Mom didn't reach for it back.

"I just want to be aware of what might happen. Remember, Jem, I'm a nurse. I can handle it." She gave me a comforting look, and I knew I could trust her. She wasn't going to freak out. She probably already knew the side effects anyway. She was just freshening up her knowledge.

Dad took her to chemo first. When they left, I prayed a Rosary for her. After an hour, I retreated to the front door and peered out the window. No one came. I took a nap then did my home strength workout, and they still didn't come home.

Right when I was finishing up a curry chicken recipe from Trader Joes, Mom and Dad came through the door. Chemo took three hours. I couldn't imagine how boring that would have been.

"We're home," Dad called through the hallway. "You did good today, Colette," I could hear him say to Mom. "Jem is making a nice meal. It will be good for you to eat something."

After Mom sat down, I called Micah from the garage and Mara who was immersed in her studies. I made sure to place the saltshaker in the middle of the table to avoid any critiques. Today, my biggest accomplishment was feeding the family.

"So, how was it?" I asked. We all wanted to know.

"Just what you'd expect. Sitting in a chair for hours hooked up to IVs. I'm so exhausted. I think I'm too tired to eat." Mom looked over her meal that I had served for her and then her eyelids closed. She didn't even try to take a bite. Her eyelids opened again. "It's been a long day, and I just have no more energy left. Can someone help me to the couch?"

Mara stood before I could and guided her to the green couch. I watched them leave and stared at my chicken curry. I didn't really want it anymore.

* * *

Chemo treatment came like a hurricane crushing Mom's energy, stealing her appetite and weakening her immune system. She was exhausted both mentally and physically every day. This made me question what the doctors were doing. But I had to have hope.

As I left for my run each morning, I'd pray that she would have a better day than the previous day. I prayed she would heal soon. When Mara joined me, I prayed in my head silently.

Within weeks, Mom started feeling better. She ate almost a normal amount, and her excitement for going on walks increased. Her mood improved the whole mood of my house, and we started laughing again. The chemo was working.

One night, I made stir fry over rice with a variety of veggies. The salt stayed in the middle of the table, so everyone would be happy. We were all in a cheery mood, especially Mom. Mom hadn't barfed in three days; we had a family lunch out on the patio, and now we were having a family dinner.

Mom was getting into more hobbies such as writing letters and creating postcards with old photos. She had mental space for creativity. Finally, she was Colette again.

Mom put her fork down on a piece of celery.

"Ah-ha! You have this veggie in here. What's this called again?" she asked.

"Celery?" Micah replied in confusion. "The veggie that doesn't taste like anything," he joked.

"Oh, right! Chemo brain!" We all laughed. Now, she had something to blame when she made a silly mistake.

"Chemo brain" became the laughingstock of the house. Every mistake Mom made or word she forgot, she blamed it on chemo.

Driving to chemo appointments soon became a natural part of Mom's weekly routine and ours as well. It became a casual conversation, as normal as chatting about the news or going shopping. Everyone understood it as a part of life with cancer.

Mom's friends would offer to accompany her on the three-hour journey. I wanted to take her at least once, so I made sure to have her reserve my spot on the calendar.

Mom recorded everything in her nine-by-twelve-inch calendar. It was her go-to tool for scheduling every appointment, phone call, and encounter. Whenever she needed to recall the last time she saw her friend Susan, she would simply flip through the months to find it.

Her handy dandy calendar kept her organized and it inspired me to keep my life organized too. I had a miniature version of her calendar hoping to be as organized as her. She was my role model in so many ways.

When it became my turn to take Mom, I laced up my shoes and threw on some sweats over my running clothes. If chemo took three hours, I knew I was going to have time to get my eight-mile run in.

I wanted to go to see firsthand what she endured for three entire hours. The building was unlike the typical hospital structure. From the outside, it resembled a commercial office building, but inside, it had the feel of a therapy clinic. It was quiet, relaxed even. We were welcomed by some nurses that Mom, of course, knew by name.

She was led to a light blue leather chair. It reminded me of the chair in a dentist's office. There was even a little tray with supplies. A nurse wheeled over a stand connected with tubes and bags filled with liquid. Mom sat on the chair and immediately opened her bag. I didn't even realize that she had swapped her normal purse with a giant blue and yellow striped beach bag. What could she have possibly brought?

The bag contained snacks, a journal, a few books, her calendar, a water bottle, the newspaper, a jacket, her headphones, and her Spotify playlists all set up on her phone. It was like she was Mary Poppins. She was going to have no trouble entertaining herself.

The nurse proceeded with the routine, gently inserting a needle in Mom's wrist. The IV tube was connected to a bag of liquid, likely containing more therapeutic substances. These chemicals caused drowsiness and fatigue, which explained why she needed assistance with transportation. As I observed the liquid flow into her body, I wondered about the specific effects of those chemicals. A shiver of nerves gave me a tickle.

I looked over at Mom. None of this phased her. She took out her calendar and pen and jotted some notes, probably writing down what time she was getting her treatment.

"Hey, Jem, I need to send some texts and schedule some things, and then I'll probably take a nap. You can go off on your run." I thought she might want to chat a little, but I figured the confines of the blue hospital chair made her want to get work done.

"Great," I replied even though I didn't want to leave her yet. "Okay. I'm going to run with my phone, so if you need anything, just give me a call. I love you." I gave her a big tight squeeze.

"I love you too. Have fun." I waved back at her as I walked down the hospital hallway. I stepped out into the parking lot and inhaled deeply. Cars hurriedly moved, their drivers heading toward unknown destinations. People walked with their phones in their hands contacting their bosses, friends, or family. Each person had a life they were living, and it struck me with a pang of sadness for my own situation. I yearned for Mom's recovery, hoping that the chemotherapy would work its magic, allowing us to return to our familiar sense of normalcy.

My college coach gave me a workout plan for the whole summer. Coach Lewis was very specific when it came to how fast my reps were, the number of miles a week I ran, and the importance of staying focused on my goals. Lately, I have been having a hard time following the plan.

I looked at my Excel spreadsheet that Coach Lewis sends weekly and saw my workout today was three miles five thirty-mile pace including a warm-up and a cool down of two miles each. After seeing Mom strapped up with needles, I had no energy or desire to run the workout. I cut myself some slack, and I decided to just run the whole eight miles at an easy pace.

Once I begin running, I thought, *I will feel much better.* I didn't. My legs felt like Jello, barely able to hold my body weight up. I felt like it could drop to the ground at any moment. I was heavy, unmotivated, and fatigued. I felt like a piece of trash.

As I continued my run, what started as a steady pace gradually deteriorated into a slow, weary jog. I passed a family laughing together setting up a picnic on a freshly mowed lawn. They embodied a happiness I so desperately craved, and the sight nearly unraveled me. I stopped my watch and collapsed my hands to my knees, my breath coming in ragged gasps. My body was drenched in sweat and fatigue, while my mind was overwhelmed with a profound, crushing sorrow.

I longed to be part of that family's effortless joy. I yearned for a life devoid of worry, where happiness was genuine and not just a facade. For weeks, our family had pretended, joking and striving for a semblance of normalcy. But beneath the surface, it was all an act—a desperate mask we wore to shield Mom from the harsh reality and to convince ourselves that everything would be alright.

I didn't want to be terrified anymore. I was tired of the constant fear and the strain it placed on our family. I wanted us to be healthy and to experience true laughter again—not the kind that masks our pain, but the kind that springs from true peace.

My emotions whirled inside me, the anger and sadness prompting my body to run again. This time, I ran faster. I soon found myself sprinting, running as fast as I could to stop the emotional anguish by turning it to physical pain.

I sprinted until I couldn't anymore. I stopped and gasped for air, leaning over the sidewalk to catch my breath. I felt so tired, but I also felt nothing. No more emotions were trapped inside. I felt relief, a small sense of freedom. Running was an escape. I glanced at my watch. A five-fifteen mile. I jogged back to the hospital with no energy left for worry.

FIVE

Aside from running, I prayed a lot.

To an outsider, it might have looked like I was chatting with the ceiling during prayer. I'd lie in bed with my back flat and hands clasped, speaking softly as if God wanted me to voice all my thoughts.

The length of my prayers depended on how much I had to say and how tired I felt from the day's events. But no matter how long it lasted, those moments were always the best part of my day. In those peaceful interludes, I tried to let go of my control, worries, and frustrations. Sometimes, I would have a sense of peace, other days, I just trusted that I would have peace, hopefully soon.

The long-awaited conversation arrived in mid-August. Faced with the decision of whether to return to school, I found myself grappling with uncertainty. Despite the challenges of chemotherapy, Mom's condition appeared to be improving, instilling in me confidence in the medical experts.

"You're going back to school," Mom insisted. "You have to go live your life. You are young. College is important to find who you are. I will not hold you back." She held out her arms for a hug, and I dropped my chest into hers.

"But, Mom," I whispered in her ear, "you are part of who I am. You're my mom. If you need me to stay here, just say the word, and I will." I gave her a kiss on the cheek. I loved her so much. Although watching her endure pain was exhausting, I would choose to be by her side any day.

"Honey, I want you to go back and train with the team and have fun. College goes by so fast. You need to be with your friends, like Sarah, and meet some boys. You need to go experience it." She gave me a wink, and I almost laughed when she said boys. I was more interested in sports than having time with dating. I did miss Sarah.

"I'm going to miss you. I'm going to keep praying for you every day, and I'll call you every day, okay?" I looked at her with puppy dog eyes. My heart was warming up inside.

"Of course. I would love that. Call me as much as you want. I will be here, probably on this couch." She grabbed me in for another hug. This one was tighter and warmer. "I love you so much, honey." I didn't want to let go.

Walking back to my room, I immediately texted my roommate Sarah.

Hey, my mom is okay with me going back to school. I'll be moving back soon. My mom wants me to meet some boys LOL.

Sarah texted back. *Anything can happen! Can't wait to see you!*

* * *

The metal gate creeped open, and I walked through the bars with my bright yellow luggage and rainbow striped pillow.

The gate and fences surrounding the home were ornamented with grape vines that provided small purple grapes, which exploded with flavor. Once, during football season, I trimmed a bunch of vines and handed out full grape bunches to cars as they sat in traffic.

I gazed up at my white rustic Oregon home. It needed a paint job, but I liked the way it was, worn and homey. There were old-fashioned flower curtains adorning each window, and there was a welcome mat that said, "Come right in." Of course, we didn't want just anyone to come right in; that would be weird. We had standards.

It was my home away from home. A flash of my home in California startled me, and I felt sad to be away. *Did I make the right decision?*

I shook my head. Mom wanted me to be here. She wanted me to have a good college experience. Listening to her is also helping her, I think.

My thoughts were interrupted by Sarah pushing the front door open.

"Hey, you're back!" She waved at me and stood on the steps.

"Sarah!" I yelled, not caring if the neighbors heard. I leaped up the two stairs to the doorway and gave her a tight hug. Sarah was shorter than me, with blonde hair an inch past her shoulders. Her eyes were as blue as sapphires, and her demeanor was calm to an outsider but to me, she was all sass.

"Looks like you slept on the plane," she speculated with some spunk. I was wearing baggy sweats and a stained gray hoodie, and my hair was half in a ponytail and half tangled by my face. It was an early morning flight, and I had no desire to look good.

"I had to get my beauty sleep in." I gave her a distorted smile, trying to mimic her sass and make her laugh. Sarah giggled and opened the door wider.

"Come in. I bet you need some tea." I followed her to the kitchen where I dropped my luggage and pillow and sat down in the kitchen nook. The nook had the best lighting because it was outlined with windows in a circular shape. The sun was able to shine through all parts of the day. It was crucial in Oregon to have windows since there were many overcast days. I sank into my seat with a deep sigh, showing that although my body had finally relaxed, my mind was still heavy with thoughts.

"I'll take green decaf. Same as you." Sarah only drank decaffeinated tea. She went off caffeine when she got too reliant on it. Green decaf was now her favorite.

She brought it over in my favorite mug. It was light purple with a big yellow sun on it. In the sun there were bold letters that read: TODAY I WILL CHOOSE JOY. It was an immediate lift to my spirits.

It was nice to be served. I realized I was serving so much at home that I had forgotten how tiring it was. Sarah handed me the mug, and its warmth sent a delightful tingle through my fingers.

"So, how's your mom?" She sat across from me, the light reflecting off her white skin. I took a sip of my tea to give me time to find the right words.

"Well, she's doing chemo now, and I hope it's able to heal her. It's too early to tell." I looked down and thought of more words to say. "She is in good spirits for the most part. And she's eating more. Everything takes time. I just have to keep praying for her. That's all I can do now."

I looked up and Sarah was staring intently at me. Her eyes were soft, and I could sense her compassionate heart had taken over.

"Jem, I'm sorry you are going through this. Please know that I am praying for her too." She smiled and reached out her hand and touched my shoulder.

I didn't want to cry, so I changed the subject. "So, what's new with you?" I asked lightheartedly.

"I got a small part-time job at the campus fitness center. I start next week. And guess what? They are hiring lifeguards at the pool!" She eyed me as if this information would excite me.

"Then you can't be lazy about working out!" I joked. Sarah had a habit of working out hard for a week or two and then tapering off.

"Yes, that's right. So given that the gym is right next to the indoor pool, you should apply to be a lifeguard." Now I understood where she was going with this.

"Why? I'm on the track team. I don't need a job that helps me workout." I took another sip of my tea.

"That's not what I mean. You should be a lifeguard because it's fun and easy, and it will distract you from everything that is going on with your mom. Since I have a job, you'll be coming home to an empty house, but if you get one too, then we will both be happily busy. And we might get to say hi to each other during our shifts."

I thought about what she said. She did have a good point. I didn't want to be alone after practice and school. I could have a job for a couple of hours a day. That did seem a little fun.

"Okay, I'll apply."

* * *

I was hired on the spot. Once my boss found out that I was on the track team and could swim, he had no doubt that I was a good match. He signed me up for lifeguard training the following weekend.

Cross Country season was just beginning, and I felt a sense of duty to make it a good one. Mom let me come back to school. She wanted me to live, to do something big. I was going to make her proud. It was going to be my fastest season yet.

The first day of practice is always fun because you get to catch up with your teammates. This time, it wasn't. I had to lie my way through the chitchat about summer. I told them the weather was nice and that I went to the beach, usual California things. I wasn't going to mention Mom. Not on the first day at least.

I chose to be the listener as we ran in a big huddle on a shaded trail. Since it was the first day of practice, it was an easy run.

"Hi, Mom, how are you feeling today?" I spoke on the phone, keeping my daily promise to check in. Hearing her voice was always comforting, though it weighed heavy on me when she was in pain.

"Much better, sweetie. I ate some toast today, and I have been getting up without help. I think my body is getting more used to chemo. Or at least my mind is." Adapting is always the hardest part of anything, and I am glad she was getting over that hump.

"That is so good to hear! Good job, Mom. I am so proud of you." Her small accomplishments were important. Each step of healing was good news.

"Yes, things are looking good. It's been a good day. Mara has been hanging out with me a lot too." Mara's school started later, so she was still taking care of mom.

A minute after we hung up, Mara texted me. *Mom just barfed. She's been barfing a lot today. I don't know whether she's going downhill, or it's just a bad day.* I gazed at the screen, torn between confusion and worry.

I thought she was having a good day? I texted back.

Mara responded. *She's protecting you.*

I flung my phone across the room, letting out a heavy sigh. What more was she hiding from me? I pressed my hands against my forehead, overwhelmed, and sighed again. My gaze fixed on the ceiling for what felt like an eternity. I was consumed by a deep, aching distress. I just wanted Mom to be okay.

I turned to prayer in my despair. "God, I miss my mom so much. Please, help her heal. I need her to get better; it breaks my heart knowing she's sick." Tears I couldn't control began to fall. "God, I know You're with her. Please stay close to her." After that, my words faltered, leaving me in a silent plea.

I remember staring at the ceiling for a while. I felt alone. I felt that it wasn't right to be away from my mom. I wanted to be by her side. But I also wanted to be here. I wanted to live my college life and reach the goals I set for myself in the upcoming track season and be with my friends. I felt torn between my priorities.

I had to take a few breaths and remember that I was where I needed to be. Mom, who was always looking out for the good of others, had encouraged me to go. She said I needed to continue my life as she slowly continued with hers.

That night, feeling a bit frustrated and negative, I took a deep breath and reminded myself that I still had a lot to be thankful for. Eventually, I drifted off to sleep, all alone on a mattress with no warmth.

* * *

Lifeguard training went by, and I had passed my test. Plus, running was going well and helped lessen my worry about Mom. I had the endorphins to thank for that. But I had also told Coach Lewis about Mom. He was sympathetic, even more than I thought, encouraging me to take my runs easy and not be in the race schedule until I was mentally okay.

All the pressure was off, but also track season was months away. I could afford to relax. My mental game was here and there. It was hard to focus on school, but my new role as a lifeguard was really good at distracting me because despite all odds, I had met a boy.

It all happened on my third day on the job.

"Hey, girl!" Gabby exclaimed with delight as I entered the lifeguard area. Her energy matched my mood.

"Hey, Gabby! It's so good to see you!" I opened my arms for a hug. After the first day of meeting Gabby, we instantly hit it off. She was upbeat and enthusiastic, and we had a common love for working out. However, she was into weightlifting, and I was into running.

"Yes! Best shift ever!" I pumped my fist in the air while I reached for the red rescue tube. I needed it when I went on duty.

Gabby was in the middle of doing a chemical check. As she filled up the test tube of pool water, I admired her gorgeous dark curly hair falling across her back and her dark skin that was glowing with a fresh tan.

"I took the five thirty morning shift, so I am off now. You are working with Dominic," she clarified. The early morning shift sounded horrible. I requested the midday shift, which was ten to three.

"Who is Dominic?" I asked thoroughly disappointed but intrigued at the same time.

"Oh, he started working here a couple months before you. I guess you've never met him. He's nice."

Gabby was drinking her energy shake, which she had pulled out of her backpack. Her black backpack matched the gym shark leggings she wore. I liked the thought that Dominic was a nice guy though I was still sad about not getting to work with her.

"Well, I guess I will see for myself." I smiled, remaining positive.

"Hey, girl, hey!" Ariana entered the breakroom, waving her hands high in jazz hands. Ariana was Gabby's sister and together, they were absolutely crazy. Ariana was joining Gabby.

"Hey! Are you guys doing legs or arms today?" I had recently found out that there are certain days to train arms and legs as if you couldn't do them on the same day. For track, we lifted twice a week doing body weight exercises for every muscle group.

"We're doing legs!" Gabby was giddy. "Lots of squats. You ready?" she asked, turning to her sister.

"I'll hold on for as long as I can," Ariana joked. Gabby was a gym regular, but Ariana on the other hand, just joined whenever she felt like it. She was more of a free spirit. I was more like Gabby, who enjoyed "getting the gains" as it is commonly phrased, every day.

"Have a killer workout!" I raised my hand up for some high fives. I wanted them to meet Sarah who managed the weight room, but she wasn't working today.

"For sure! See you in a bit." Gabby and Ariana left the lifeguard area. When she left, I peered out to the pool area. I could see the back of Dominic's hair. It was dirty brown. I could also see that his skin was pale, and he was tall. Very tall. Maybe as tall as Micah.

At the top of the hour, I walked onto the pool deck to trade places with Dominic. I casually waved and smiled at the regular swimmers while I made my way to the lifeguard chair. I mumbled a little prayer for the swimmers. No one was going to drown on my watch if I could help it.

"Hi, I'm Jem. I'm a new lifeguard." I introduced myself to Dominic. I stood by the nine-foot lifeguard chair as he stepped down. He stood up, and I silently affirmed myself for getting his height right. He was about six foot four, same height as Micah. Dominic was very lean, a body that was healthy and quite attractive. I tried not to blush.

When he turned his head toward me, I could see that his light brown eyes matched the freckles on his nose. He was a cutie, but he wasn't my cutie, so I tried to act normal. I looked away to release tension and focus on the swimmers.

"Hey, Jem. I'm Dominic," he said without a smile. I nodded. I didn't have time to read into the lack of smile on his face because I was now on the job. I took lifeguarding very seriously.

My gaze went from the lap pool to the hot tub and then to the dive pool and back. I noticed that Dominic hadn't left. He was still standing next to me. Thinking that was odd, I did what I always did in awkward situations, I talked.

"I'm surprised you don't wear sandals," I joked. I glanced down at his feet, and he had these black Asics on that were tied in double knots. It was silly to me to have shoes on when you might have to jump in the water at any moment.

I wore turquoise slides that said "stay cool" on them with bright pink lettering. The bright colors made me smile.

"You're right; I shouldn't be wearing these. It's silly, isn't it?" I could see a little smirk emerge from his lips. "I would definitely wear those shoes if they had them in my size." He admired my slides. That made me laugh.

"Yeah, I mean, two strong flips of my feet and these sandals are flying off. Nothing is holding me back from saving a life."

I looked over at him with my eyebrows raised to get my point across. He was smiling. He must have thought I was amusingly annoying.

"Jem, how are you so happy?" He stared at me as if I was inhuman.

Before I could even think, I said what was truly in my heart. "Because I love Jesus," I answered. I wasn't sure if I was allowed to say that at work, but I did. I wouldn't be happy without Jesus because he gave me hope. *And hope does not disappoint.*

"Oh." He seemed stumped. I didn't really know how to reply to that.

"Yeah, I'm Catholic. I had a deep experience of Jesus's love a year ago in the Catholic Mass, and I've been a believer ever since. But I also know that Jesus works wherever you are as long as you let him in." I didn't know why I was revealing this all to him. Dominic was basically a stranger to me.

We stood there for a couple of moments, and I could tell that Dominic was really thinking.

"Can I go to church with you?" he asked, interrupting the silence. Dominic peered at me with puppy dog eyes. I thought it was precious.

"Yes, of course, you can. I am going on Sunday at ten thirty. It's called Saint Mary's."

"I live right by it." Dominic looked excited, which made me excited. I wanted him to know Jesus. He stood next to me, and we chatted the rest of the shift.

I couldn't believe I had met a boy. What were *Dominic's intentions? Did Dominic want to go to church to know Jesus or did he want to go to church to know me? Or was it both?* I liked the sound of that. I had to figure it out before I made any dumb moves. I wondered what Mom would say.

Later that day, Mara called me. She had just got off her flight. Mara had returned to college, so she wasn't there to be the caregiver. Her school was on semester system, so they started later. Mara felt okay about leaving because the chemotherapy treatment was almost done, and Mom was responding well to it. There was no more barfing, and Mom was managing all her daily tasks with no help.

"I miss Mom already." She sighed into the phone. I knew exactly how she felt.

"I miss her too. But we will see her in no time. Christmas break will be here before we know it." I tried to be optimistic, but it was only September, and that was four months away.

"How do you focus on school?" she asked, wanting to know the secret. There weren't any.

"I don't," I replied honestly. "I blank randomly thinking of Mom and then I focus again, and I am lost." I was surprised that I was passing my classes, but I currently have a C in psychology. "Honestly, sis, you're going to do much better than me. Fortunately, I have teachers who post their PowerPoints, so I am getting by with that information."

"Okay, well I guess I'll just find a way to block it out," she responded. I could tell she was not happy with my answer. But there wasn't really one. There is no way to avoid the thought that Mom has cancer, and she could possibly not survive. I couldn't even think about that. She wasn't going to die. Surely, she'd press through.

"You'll be fine! You are the amazing, Mara; you work so hard, and it's going to pay off, no doubt!" I felt a deep urgency to become her cheerleader, desperately trying to shift her focus away from my own troubled thoughts. I was rallying for both of us, hoping to boost her confidence in her classes and distract us from the fact that we left our sick mom at home.

* * *

It was already Sunday morning, and I had a harder time picking out my outfit than usual. It seemed important that I looked good for Dominic, but in the big picture, I was dressing up for Jesus. He is the one that I was really going for.

I went for the simple look of a black skirt and a gray top and my hair down. With a straightener, I erased the random waves in my hair I got from sleeping. I put on my nice white dress shoes that looked like a nicer version of Converse. I smiled in the mirror, and I grabbed my bag that held my journal, a pen, my phone, and a tissue just in case I cried or had a runny nose.

Dominic was already there when I arrived. It was ten minutes until mass started. He was wearing khaki pants, a white T-shirt with a short sleeve checkered button-up that was left unbuttoned. It made me giggle a little. At least he was trying.

I stepped out of my car and gave him a wave. He waved back and smiled. When I approached him, I wasn't sure what to do but when his arms opened, I knew that there was a cue to go in for a hug.

"Hi!" I exclaimed in my normal happy tone but abnormally happy to those that don't know me.

"Hey, Jem!" His smile was charming. *Okay, stop it, Jem! You are here for Jesus. Yay Jesus!* I faced the church doors.

"Come on, let's find a seat. Follow me." It was important to me to get there early, so I could gather myself and say a few quick prayers. That way, I could be in the proper headspace before mass began.

I strolled into Saint Mary's and used my lifeguard gaze to scan for open seats. I usually sat extremely close to the front—the place where many people didn't dare go. I liked being in the front because there were no distractions, and I could truly focus on the celebration of the sacrifice.

Being prudent, I chose a pew that was in the middle section. I glanced back to see if Dominic was still behind me. Out of the corner of my eye, I saw a group of my church friends giving us a stare-down. I knew exactly what they were thinking. I had a boyfriend. Girls didn't take random guys to mass. Except for me. I tried to shrug it off, and I leaned over to Dominic.

"Is this spot, okay?"

"Yeah," he answered and followed me into the section.

"Hey, so I am going to go on my knees to say a little prayer before church begins. You can stay seated in the pew if you want." I listened for a reply, but he just nodded. I think he was scared to talk.

He looked at me. "What's the pew?" he whispered.

"It's the seat," I whispered back. Then I turned forward to focus on Jesus. There was a giant image of the crucified Jesus behind the altar. Many churches had them. Ours was different because if you looked closely Jesus was not nailed to the cross; He was floating a little bit in front of it to symbolize the resurrection. To me, the image was more hopeful.

I also enjoyed staring at the candles when I prayed. Something about the flicker of fire calmed me. Everything about the Catholic church was intentional and symbolic, something that sparked a sense of wonder inside me. There was so much meaning behind it all. Maybe one day Dominic will understand it too.

I begin to pray. I asked Jesus if He would calm my heart and Dominic's heart. I prayed for Mom that she would continue getting stronger from her chemotherapy. I wanted her to receive peace and healing.

The music started, and the Mass was in session. I had forgotten to explain to Dominic the order of the Mass. I had also forgotten to tell him we sit and stand throughout the celebration. The worst part about taking someone new to church is that they get confused, and people do not like being confused. I think that's why a lot of people don't turn to faith.

"Hey," I leaned in toward him so he could hear me. I felt like a child talking over the music. "There is a whole order to the Mass, and there are prayers we recite; I can explain it all later but for now, you can just follow my lead." He nodded.

I surrendered my prayers and focused on Jesus, allowing the music, readings, and sacrifice to deeply engage my soul.

When the service ended, I looked at Dominic trying to gauge his impression of the Mass. He had a neutral expression. But he did look content.

"What did you think?" I asked him as we were walking out.

"It was very calming." He followed me out of the doors where a bunch of college-age kids were chatting. I knew almost all of them.

My friend John came marching up to us. John was extremely friendly and loved to talk to others about faith. I could see him being a missionary one day.

"Hey, Jem!" he called out to me.

"Hey, John!" We pumped our fists together in all directions and high-fived in three different ways. It was a handshake that we made up months ago, but we made it our thing. I was surprised we both didn't forget it over summer vacation.

"This is my friend Dominic," I said as I introduced him. It was easier to introduce him as a friend than as an acquaintance.

"Hey, man; it's good to meet you. Are you Catholic?" John was so bold.

"My parents are. Well, they were. They don't go to church anymore," Dominic answered. This was information I didn't know. It was common for parents these days to stop going to church in a world that was so anti-faith.

"Nice. I am glad you are coming back. I would love to answer any questions you have regarding Catholicism." John grinned in an inviting way. He had an easy time charming people. After that, he walked away and left us alone. We stood there awkwardly for a moment.

"Thanks for letting me come. What are you doing now?" Dominic asked.

In my head, Dominic was joining me for church. That was it. I froze in my tracks. I was not the spontaneous type.

"Well, do you want to go on a walk?" I was quick to respond. It was a beautiful summer day. A walk was always a good option. Everything was in bright colors.

Dominic's eyebrows raised. "Sure. Wherever you go, I'll go."

Walking was one of my hobbies. To an outsider, I was boring. In my opinion, walking was never boring.

There's so much to explore on a walk—everything from quirky house designs to the peacefulness of nature, not to mention the delightful endorphin boost to your brain. I could stroll around all day, every day. We decided to check out a nearby park that I often glimpsed during my runs.

"So, uh your parents are Catholic?" I asked as we strolled. I was curious to know his background.

"Yeah, they are Catholic and got married in the church, but they haven't been to church in a really long time. I haven't been either, so it was nice to go today." Dominic brushed his arm against mine. My stomach did a somersault.

"Well, you can come again if you want. The invitation is open," I said, truly meaning it.

"Yes, I would like to. Are your parents Catholic?" He tilted his head and looked me in the eyes.

"My mom is, but she doesn't go anymore now that she's sick." I felt so comforted by his presence that I let myself be vulnerable. Before he could speak, I continued. "She has ovarian cancer. She's currently going through chemotherapy." My smile was gone, and I felt a desire to cry.

Empathy filled Dominic's eyes, casting them with a shade of sadness. "I'm so sorry, Jem; that must be hard."

My gaze drifted to the ground. I observed the dead patches of lawn, the somber brown circles in a vibrant green field, an image to resemble my current mood.

"Yeah, it's really hard." I sniffed a little, holding in my tears. "That's why I like church so much. It's the one place I know I will find peace. Praying is the one thing that I can do for my mom and for myself. Praying is healing." I believed that praying healed even if God was just healing our souls.

"I also like to pray the rosary for her," I added. My eyes began to well up again. In a moment, I was back next to my mom in the hospital bed, seeing her scarred from surgery, almost lifeless, and completely helpless. I shook my head to erase those thoughts. She was much better now; Mara had told me. She was eating and walking and laughing. I missed her.

I felt Dominic's warm hand on my back, and I let myself lean into his chest. The safety of his chest made me want to stay there forever.

The swings at the playground were vacant. We swung a few times while watching the empty blue sky sit in the air with confidence. We stayed there, swinging silently until my tears had dried.

In time, I let my swing sway to a stop, and I gazed at Dominic indicating I was ready to break the silence. He slowed his swing and gave me a half smile.

"Thanks for being patient. Sometimes, the tears come, and I have no control."

"Why don't we get some lunch," Dominic suggested. "It might cheer you up a little."

I jumped off the swing with a grateful heart. I was grateful for Dominic.

"Yes, please. I know the best burger place."

That evening, I called my mom. I had a lot to tell her. Usually, it would be the same old thing. I would describe my running workouts and tell her how I was feeling. I would tell her something about my classes or a joke I heard. Now, I could tell her I met a boy.

"I met some guy at work, and he wanted to go to church with me," I explained, trying not to sound too excited. "And he actually came, and he liked it. Then he took me out to lunch."

"Oh, honey, that is so wonderful!" She sounded extremely happy for me, and I could imagine her smile going up to her ears. "Is he cute?"

"Yes, he is!" I squealed. "I think he likes me, but I'm not sure." I was pacing around my room matching the butterflies in my stomach. This boy stuff was new.

"Well, what's his name?" she asked, fully immersed in our conversation.

"Dominic. I really like it. His name means 'belonging to God.' I researched it this afternoon." I liked that his name had a deeper meaning even if he didn't know it.

"That's lovely, Jem. I hope that things continue to go well with him. I am just so happy for you!"

"Yeah, me too." I beamed. "And how are you? Do you miss Mara?" I plopped my butt on the end of my bed ready to focus on her.

"I am doing pretty good. I do miss Mara and you. I'm feeling tired but not too tired. I took a nap today, and Rita came over for a bit. We talked the day away. Rita has been coming over more." Rita was mom's sister, and she was a firecracker. She was brutally honest and extremely talkative. They were best friends.

Once I got off the phone, I stood up and jumped backward onto my bed. I flopped down in a giant star position. I felt like a star too. I was elated. Mom had a good day, and I had a crush.

SIX

A couple days later, I was back out on lifeguard duty humming to the song *Invisible Touch* by Genesis. I loved cranking '80s music. It wasn't just me—people from the older generation were equally hooked. We had an indoor pool equipped with speakers, and playing music was definitely one of the highlights of the job.

It had been a week, and Dominic hadn't asked me out again, so I figured he just wanted to be friends. And if that's what he wanted, then it was fine with me too. I had a lot on my plate, so it was better that I didn't have boy drama.

Dominic crept up behind me and tapped me with his lifeguard buoy.

"Hey."

"Hello, good morning! Happy Friday!" I cheered. It was going to be a good day. I ran while watching the sunrise this morning, and I still felt high.

Dominic looked nervous. "I got you a gift."

"A gift?" I asked. I needed to make sure I was hearing him right. There was nothing in his hands but the rescue tube.

"Yeah, I got you something. I put it in your backpack in the break station. It matches your eyes." He swayed his weight back and forth on each foot.

It wasn't my birthday, and it wasn't a holiday. Maybe Dominic did like me. Boys don't give girls gifts for no reason.

"Wow, thanks! I will open it now." I left him to watch the water and made my way into the station. I unzipped my bag and saw a cloth drawstring pouch. It felt heavy in my hand.

I untied the drawstring and pulled out a Rosary. The sky-blue colored beads were mesmerizing, and I held my breath at the sight of this beautiful item. My eyes welled up with appreciation. I blinked back the tears and peered through the glass at Dominic. I mouthed the words *thank you* and then sat back in my chair.

The Rosary felt like it was meant for me. If I could choose any color beads it would be this shade. I loved sky blue and so did my mom. My favorite shirt was sky blue, a hand-me-down from my mom. To me, it was a hopeful color.

I let the Rosary fall between my fingers as my other hand caught it from underneath. It was as if I was holding sand, inhaling the texture, and letting the sense of touch take over. It was by far the greatest gift I had ever received.

Later that day, I clutched the cobalt Rosary in my hand as I walked home from work. The twenty-minute stroll provided the perfect opportunity for prayer, as it matched the time it took to say the Rosary.

I let my mind relax as I prayed each Hail Mary. For the first time in a while, it felt easier to breathe. I was surrendering everything I had to the prayer. Everything within me felt lighter while the Rosary felt powerful in my palm.

When I got home, I kicked my shoes off, grabbed an apple from the fridge, and called Mom. Parading out to my deck, I chomped down on the tasty Golden Delicious. I clicked my phone on the speaker and smiled at the sun.

"Hey!" Mom exclaimed through the phone.

"Hi, Mommy! How are you doing?" I asked, hoping she was having another good day.

"You know, Jem, my day wasn't going so well, but just recently I have been feeling a strong sense of peace."

"You have?" I asked, trying not to get too excited.

"Yeah, it was crazy; it kinda just took over. I am feeling very grateful right now." Mom's voice was smooth and relaxed.

I mouthed *thank you* to the sky hoping Jesus was watching.

"Get this, Mom. I was just praying for you. On my way home, I was praying. Right before I called."

"Well, isn't that something?" she answered, mulling it over in her head.

After our conversation, I felt a surge of adrenaline to look up flights home. What if I surprised her? I missed her and wanted to be in her presence. I could manage getting shifts covered and missing classes. Plus, I could run from anywhere; surely the team wouldn't miss me. A couple days wouldn't hurt anyone—it would only help!

I found a flight for the next day and booked it immediately. Then I sent a text to Dad. He was on board with making it a surprise. It was hard to keep the jitters from showing.

Back on the lifeguard stand, I was smiling wide, and nothing could ruin it. Betty, an elderly lady who came to swim once a week, was here. She hobbled over to me with a big smile on her face. Her hair, styled in a white bob, tickled her cheekbones. She held a cane in her right hand and wore a one-piece light pink bathing suit with red roses on it. On her feet, she had black flip flops.

"Jem, darling," she said with ease. "How good it is to see your face. Will you help me get into the pool?"

"Good morning, Betty. Of course I can help you. It's a great day for a swim." Her usual spot was the shallow end where there was a rail and stairs. Once she got in her place, I took the cane from her hand and set it against the far wall where people left their towels.

I came back over to her and flipped my slides off as she did the same. I held onto her left hand as she held the rail with her right. We went down one step at a time until she reached the four-foot floor.

"Thank you, Jem. You are such a big help."

"No worries, Betty. You have a good swim now. I'll be right here." I gave her a big, animated smile and a wave and walked back to my lifeguard stand. I watched her dog-paddle with pure enjoyment. I was proud of her for exercising at her age.

I admired her light pink swimsuit with roses on it. Another secret reminder to me to pray a Rosary later.

Before long, Dominic emerged from the lifeguard station to switch me out. Again, he was working the same shift as me. We were getting lucky. However, I had seen our boss give us some glances, and I knew he was putting the pieces together.

"Good morning!" I chimed a little too loudly. My morning energy was really coming through.

"Hey, Jem," Dominic said half asleep. It was eleven by now, but I could sense that he had just woke up. I had already run five miles before the shift.

"Hey, I just want to say thank you so much for the Rosary. It is the most meaningful gift I have ever received. It's beautiful."

"You're welcome. I hoped you would like it. I got one for myself too. Maybe you can teach me how to pray with it." He seemed very genuine and open to learning about my faith.

"Yes, of course, I can teach you how to pray with it. But you probably need to learn a little bit more about Catholicism first or it won't make sense. Little by little." At first, the Rosary was hard for me to wrap my head around until I was taught the meaning of each prayer. That's when the joy of asking Mary to pray for you comes alive. It is kinda like with everything, if there is meaning to it, it comes alive.

"Speaking of the Rosary," I continued, "I prayed for my mom yesterday, and then I talked to her, and she was in such a good headspace! Then later, I had this thought. Why don't I visit her and make it a surprise? And so, I bought my ticket for tonight!" I wanted to do a little dance but held back.

"Wow, that's thoughtful," he said, still sounding sleepy and staring off into the distance. I didn't know whether he was still trying to wake up or he was sad that I was leaving. "How long are you going for?"

"Three nights." There was a lull of silence. It seemed like my cue to leave.

"Well, I'm going to go take my break," I said excusing myself, and I started walking away.

"Wait! Jem, can I have your number, so I can text you?"

"Sure. I'll write it down in the break room." I sauntered off happily that he wanted my number. It was about time he asked.

SEVEN

When I entered the door of my childhood home, I went straight for the bedroom. My instincts told me Mom was there. She was folding her laundry when I bounced in. I stood there motionless.

"Hey, Mom," I said casually standing by the doorway. Mom peered up, and when she recognized what was happening, she screamed.

"Jem! Oh, my gosh!" I could already see happy tears well up in her eyes. I ran over to her and gave her a hug.

"Jem, you're here!" she exclaimed, still in amazement. Still hugging, we both started jumping up and down with joy and making noises that could resemble squealing pigs.

Dad stood in the doorway. "Alright. The surprise has been had. So happy to have you back, Jem." He patted me on the back and then left us alone for our girl time.

Mom and I stopped jumping and I gazed at the joy on her face. It was worth coming home. I didn't even care if I went back to school. I opened my arms and hugged her again, this time without squealing. I rubbed her back and felt the divots of her backbone. She had lost more weight.

I stepped back so I could assess her. I noticed she was wearing a beanie.

"Are you cold?" I asked. It was early fall, but the days were slightly getting colder. Still, it wasn't cold, and neither was our house.

"Well, yes and no." She looked at me seriously. "There is something I want to tell you." She held her hand on her head like she was going to reveal something. My mind went from A to Z in a heartbeat. Chemo had zapped her hair; she was bald.

The beanie slid off her clean head. It was so shiny and spotless. Her head was the most perfectly bald head I had ever seen. It looked unreal.

My jaw dropped open the second the beanie was off. Then I felt the need to give her another big hug. And then, like most five-year-olds, I wanted to touch it. I reached my hand to her scalp and rubbed my palm over it. It was incredibly sleek. I was also shocked. Even though bald, she was still beautiful. It was both remarkable and fascinating.

"Whoa, Mom, you're really bald. Like completely bald. Not like Dad bald but bald bald." My speech was engrossed with saying the word *bald*.

"I know; it's all gone! And smooth. Isn't it fun to touch?"

"Yeah! It's addicting." I grazed my palm around her cranium for the third time.

Usually, you don't notice baldness because it's older men who have it. It's the natural aging process. But here my mom was fifty-seven years old. It was definitely out of place.

Honestly, Mom rocked the bald look. I was amazed at how her hairless head gave her this androgynous model vibe. I couldn't resist snapping a photo with her.

"You better not show that to anyone."

"Why not, Mom? You look great bald!" I reassured her.

She sighed and sat down on the edge of her bed. "Jem, I don't want to be bald. I want to have hair. I don't want to look sick."

She was right. Nobody her age would shave their head as a hairstyle. It was obvious she was sick. If she took her beanie off in public, people would know she had cancer.

"I'm sorry you don't like it. Just remember that I like it, and I think you could be a model. It could be your new career." I needed to reassure her that she wasn't ugly.

"Well thanks, honey. I'm actually looking at wigs. I have a friend who has an extra wig, and she is going to bring it over this week."

"That's exciting, Mom. New hair, who this?" I joked. It made sense that she would want a wig to help her feel normal. You don't really know what normal feels like until you aren't anymore.

"I hopefully won't need it that long. It should grow back soon. My first round of the chemotherapy process ended last week."

"That's very right! Now let's head over to the kitchen. I think Dad is done with dinner."

The three of us had dinner that night, completely happy enjoying each other's company.

I awoke the next morning, and I literally jumped out of bed. I was excited to kick back, relax and enjoy the whole day with Mom. I slipped out of bed early for a run, so I wouldn't miss a moment with her. Before heading out, I checked my phone. I got a text from an unknown number.

Hey, Jem, this is Dominic. How's your mom? I hope you're having a fun time.

He was checking in on me. How sweet. I typed back.

Hi! I'm having a wonderful time so far! Can't wait to see what's in store for today! By the way, my mom is bald, but she rocks it! Have a good day at work!

I was so happy I didn't even overthink my overuse of exclamation marks. I threw my phone on the bed. I didn't need music for my run. I could run off the happy energy in my veins. I laced up my shoes and headed out.

When I got back from my run, I saw a short brown-haired lady standing at our doorstep. I didn't recognize her. Mom was in the doorway chatting with her and holding a plate of cookies.

I lingered beside the Acura in our driveway and did some leg swings to loosen up. I wasn't used to holding onto the car while doing them, so I banged my foot on the tire. There was no pain, but it made a loud sound. Both Mom and the brown-haired lady turned their heads.

"Hi!" I waved trying not to be awkward.

"This is my daughter, Jem. She surprised me with a visit!" That was my cue to come shake her hand.

"Hey, sorry I'm sweaty. Nice to meet you." I decided not to shake her hand. Instead, I smiled wide and wiped the sweat off my upper lip.

"Hi, Jem. I'm Carmen. Nice to meet you too." She sounded sweet. "Well, I just wanted to stop by quickly and to check in on you. I'll let you get back to family time." She smiled politely and gave Mom another hug.

"Thanks so much for stopping by. Don't be a stranger!" It was Mom's way of asking her to come by again.

When I got back in the house, I flung off my shoes and started my stretching routine on the hallway carpet. I had a good view of the kitchen and my dad at his desk. Mom set the cookies on the countertop.

"Hey, babe, Carmen made chocolate chip cookies." She didn't touch them. She retreated into the pantry and came out holding a hamster cage.

"What the heck is that?" I asked. There was no way it was a hamster cage. We had no pets.

"It's my juicer!" she exclaimed as if it were a fancy pair of Lululemon leggings she was gifting me. Except that it wasn't exciting at all.

"Why is it so big?" She set it down on the counter, and it took up as much space as two baking trays.

"Well, it has to have room to chomp up all the fruits and veggies I'm going to put in it." She started wiping down the machine with a dry rag.

"How long have you had this?" I didn't remember her telling me about a hamster cage juicer on the phone.

"About two weeks. I have been making lots of concoctions." She smirked, trying to be witch-like.

"What are you making today?" I asked as I did a lunge stretch on the carpet.

"Beet and celery juice. My first time with beets." The bulky two-foot juicer machine made a robust sound as it chomped down on the beets and celery Mom fed it. The purple liquid that came forth from the machine looked like something you would get from a swamp in a horror film.

I abandoned my stretches and went to watch the liquid pour out. I decided that the scary movie would be called *The Juicer*. People would get their guts juiced. I instantly imagined a hamster running in the tubes of the juicer and then getting squashed to death.

I was glad there was no hamster, and I was glad that Dad interrupted my random dark thoughts.

"Mmmm, these cookies are good. Hey, Champ, you got to take some of these back to Oregon with you. I can't eat these all by myself." He was holding a half-eaten cookie while wearing his 49ers hoodie and jeans.

Dad frequently referred to me as "Champ." It was a term of endearment reserved just for me. It not only made me feel cherished but also fueled my determination to sprint even faster on the track.

"Sure, I can take some back with me. Wait, is Mom not eating them?" Confusion struck me once again. Mom loved her sweets. She loved her cookies and cakes. She even had the benefit of them passing through her metabolism without harm.

The purple beet juice was half drunk. Mom had a light residue of purple on her teeth. I wanted to laugh, but I was preoccupied with my mother's lack of sweets intake.

"Jem, I am taking a break from sweets. I need all the nutrients I can get. My body does not need sweets right now. I have to fight cancer the best I can."

Before I could respond with my suggestion that she should just eat half of a cookie instead of a whole, she launched into her next thought.

"By the way, that reminds me I have to take my vitamins." She set her beet juice on the counter and went to the pantry. I was curious to see what new device she would pull out next.

In a large cardboard tray, the ones you get from Costco, were a multitude of pill bottles. She set the box on the counter, taking up the other half of the counter, and started reading the labels.

Before I could ask what all the bottles were, she went into nurse mode. "I take a bunch of pills every morning and every night. I take them with a little bit of food; that way they can go down better, and the vitamins can activate. Beet juice is perfect for the job." She started opening up medicine bottles. I scanned the bottles, and I could see she had every vitamin possible.

I walked into the pantry while she was doing her thing. I saw there was one full shelf devoted to stashing her pills. On another shelf, I located a bunch of powders I'd never seen before. There was turmeric powder, matcha powder, beet powder, and more. There were about seven bags total.

There was no doubt that Mom wasn't skipping out on any nutrients. I could guarantee that she could check vitamin A–Z off the checklist. I walked back to Mom and observed the twenty-plus colorful pills in her hand that she swallowed in two gulps. It was impressive.

"Can you spare a multivitamin?" I asked. Her vitamin intake made me want some, and I knew she had enough.

"Of course. You need your vitamins too," she responded as she gulped down another set of pills. I grabbed the multivitamin and shook two pills in my hand. I swallowed one with a glass of water and then walked over to Dad.

"Here, Dad. You need your vitamins." I turned back to Mom. "Okay enough popping pills like you're in a nightclub. Let's go on a walk."

Later that afternoon, Mom and I read. I sat in her recliner, and she was sprawled out on the obnoxious green couch. I felt very relaxed. We were finally enjoying ourselves without having to think about cancer. Until, that is, we weren't.

"Jem, can you pass me my beanie? My head is getting cold."

"Of course." I walked to her room and grabbed her deep magenta beanie. When I turned around, Mom was standing in the doorway. She scampered past me and kneeled down by her bed.

"I forgot that I have to do my mistletoe shot." She was searching under the bed for something.

"Mistletoe shot?" All I could think of was Christmas.

"I've been doing a lot of research, and the mistletoe shot is supposed to help with healing. It's all natural, no chemicals. I thought that I might as well do this on top of chemo. I want to try everything possible to get rid of this."

She finally found what she was looking for. It was a small black briefcase that looked secretive. Mom opened it up and it contained a set of needles. It made me think of getting my flu shot.

Trying to wrap my head around the mistletoe business, I asked her for clarity. "Mom, you're going to inject mistletoe by yourself?" I gave her a raised eyebrow.

"Exactly. Like I said, it's natural, so it won't hurt me. It could only help. Don't worry about the needles. They don't scare me. Remember, I'm a nurse." She gave me a wink.

Mom lay on the light brown duvet cover and rolled up her shirt.

"Now, Jem. I'm going to shoot it in my stomach. All you have to do is keep talking to me, so you will distract me from the pain." I nodded amidst the pressure I felt to keep her calm.

I sat down on the bed beside her feet. "So, Mom, you know that guy who went to church with me. Well, he got me a light blue Rosary because it matches my eyes, and he knows I'm Catholic. It's become my favorite thing. It was the same Rosary that I prayed for you with. I like it a lot because he thought of me when he bought it, which means he probably thought of Jesus too. I also like it because I love blue, and I know your favorite color is blue too, so it's just perfect."

Mom was smiling at me. The needle was already back in the briefcase, and her shirt was rolled back down.

"Wow, that was fast!" I was shocked to see that it was already over.

"Yep. Quick and easy! So, this guy you like believes in Jesus?"

"I hope he does. I want everyone to. He went to church with me, so he wants to believe. He said he wanted to come with me again." I thought of Dominic on the lifeguard stand. I wondered if he was thinking about anything we had talked about. I also wondered if he was thinking of me.

"Are there any other shots that you have to take that you haven't told me about?" I asked, wanting to divert the conversation so my brain wouldn't spiral about Dominic.

Mom respected my decision to switch topics. "You know when I said I'm giving up sweets? Well, that means chocolate too."

"What?! Not dark chocolate! It's healthy!" I argued. Mom loved dark chocolate. Our whole family did. A couple bites of dark chocolate chips were part of our daily routine.

"That's just what I'm doing for now. Food is medicine, and chocolate just doesn't have the nutrients I need to fight cancer." Even though I didn't agree with her, I wanted to support her. I took a pillow from the bed and hit her shoulder playfully.

"Okay, be like that. I'll just enjoy your portion of chocolate," I joked. We both giggled and started play-fighting on the bed. I went easy on her since she was in a weaker state. She managed to blow on my stomach and make a farting noise. A perfectly happy reminder of when I was a child even when sometimes, I still felt like one.

Later that evening, I finally checked my phone. I was having so much fun with Mom I had tossed my phone away and forgotten about it. However, I didn't forget who might send me a message. I checked my phone, and my heart lit up when I saw Dominic's name on the screen.

Hey, I've been thinking of you. How was your day today?

My stomach twisted into a knot. Dominic was thinking about me. This must be a sign that he somewhat had a crush on me, but I still couldn't assume.

I've been having such a great time with my mom. It's sad that I have to leave her tomorrow.

Within two minutes, Dominic replied.

I bet your mom is really enjoying your presence. I bet you are making her so happy. You make so many people happy, like me. I can pick you up from the airport if you need.

He could not have been sweeter. I sat there and read the message over three times. My stomach stayed in a knot, but it was a happy knot.

I was going to ask Sarah for a ride, but I guess I didn't need to. It was very nice of him to offer even before he knew the time of my flight. I texted back to confirm.

That would be amazing! I get into Portland at 10:20 a.m. I am going to bed now. Goodnight! :)

I set my iPhone on my old bookcase. I didn't need to charge my phone because I hardly used it. I turned on my left side and tried to sleep with the butterflies in my stomach. I didn't want to leave my mom, but at least I had something to look forward to.

The next morning, Dad urged us to leave ten minutes before the time we agreed on. He was nervous that the security lines would be long. Before following him to the driveway, I crept back into Mom's room to say goodbye.

I tiptoed to the right side of the bed and leaned toward her ear to whisper. "Good morning, Mommy. I'm leaving now with Dad. I want you to keep up the good spirits, okay? I'll be praying for you. I love you so much." I kissed her on the cheek, and she opened her eyes.

"Hug?" she asked. I was more than willing to grant her request. I pressed my heart into her chest and gave her a little squeeze. I wanted to stay there, but Dad knocked on the door frame.

"Come on, Champ." I looked up back at him and then back at Mom.

"Got to go now. I'll call you tonight." I kissed her cheek again and shuffled out of the room.

I tapped my pants pocket to make sure my phone was there, and I hopped into the car. The next time I would see Mom would be in December.

When I arrived at the Portland airport, I went straight to the pickup area to find Dominic in front of his dark gray Jeep Cherokee holding a bundle of red roses. I was shocked.

"Welcome back. I got these for you." He handed me the flowers. He looked nervous.

"These are beautiful!" I exclaimed. "I love flowers!" I sniffed them with all my might and beamed. They smelled fresh and delightful. Nerves electrified up my spine.

Before I realized it, I was giving him a hug. After a wonderful but emotional visit with Mom, this was the perfect surprise. A friend with flowers was just what I needed. Or was it a crush? I still needed clarity. Red roses made me positively suspicious.

"Thank you so much, Dominic. I will admire them every time I see them. And thank you so much for picking me up from the airport." Dominic mirrored my expression with a big smile.

"Of course, Jem. It is my pleasure. I find it very easy being around you. You are very happy even when you are going through something so hard." Now, he was the one beaming in front of me. I felt overly flattered, and I didn't know what to say.

"I'd rather be happy than be sad," was all I could muster up.

"Well then, I'm glad you choose to be happy." He was staring at me now like he wanted to kiss me, but I wasn't sure.

"Shall we?" I say pointing to the car and ignoring any signal that I thought meant kissing.

"Oh, yes . . . right," he mumbled and walked toward the driver's seat. I flung my bag in the backseat and hopped into the passenger seat with the roses. I wanted to smell them all the way home.

Roses, yet another reminder of purity, love, and sorrow from our Holy Mother. I was told by a religious sister that every time I prayed a Hail Mary, I was giving a rose to Mary. Therefore, praying the Rosary was like giving a whole bouquet of roses—fifty roses worth! I wanted to share my thoughts with Dominic.

"Do you know that Mary loves roses?" I asked him. Dominic kept his eyes on the road as he answered.

"Who's Mary?"

"Mary, the mother of God. If you pray the Rosary, you are not only sending up prayers, but you are giving her spiritual roses!"

"Oh, that's very nice." He said it in a way that I knew meant he didn't understand. "How do you know that?" he asked.

"Well, if you look online there are various accounts of people who pray the Rosary, and they actually smell the scent of roses around them even when they aren't even near a rose bush. It's incredible." I sniffed my roses again, so I could know the smell if that ever happened to me.

"Why do you think that happens?" Dominic asked, still staring ahead.

I went with the answer that seemed most obvious. "Because Mary loves us, and we are her children! And when anyone sees a rose, they immediately think of love." It made me happy saying it out loud. The conversation was making me more aware of the goodness of God.

Before Dominic could say anything, I wanted to explain further.

"Many people do not understand Mary. I don't know why. Catholics believe that Mary is our spiritual Mother. When we pray the Rosary, we are asking Mary to pray for us. We are asking Mary to help us. After all, she is with Jesus in Heaven."

I glanced at Dominic, and he seemed to be processing his thoughts. I decided to continue.

"It doesn't mean we don't go to Jesus with our prayers. It's that we can also ask Mary to pray for us too. Then it's just more prayers. And the more prayers the merrier!" I wanted to jump out of my seat, but my seatbelt held me in place.

Realizing that silence meant more confusion I took a deep breath and remained calm. I had just told him a lot of stuff. I needed to not get ahead of myself.

"It might not make much sense now, but as you grow in your faith and prayer life, it will," I reassured him. "The more you draw near to him the more, he draws near to you." I pulled that straight from James 4:8, hoping it would provide Dominic some wisdom.

"It seems like you're really good at this stuff," he finally responded.

"I wouldn't say I'm good at being religious, I would say that faith is important to me, so I invest time into knowing more about it. Anyone can pray. There is no right way or wrong way to pray. You just have to speak from the heart." I smelled my roses again.

"In that case, I'd like to pray. I think I have before. I just need to do it more."

"Great!" I answered. I was delighted that he was open to the idea. I smiled at him when he looked at me. We drove for a couple moments in silence, the air circled around us.

"You said that you invest time into things that are important. And I was thinking that I would like to invest in spending time with you." He weaved that into the conversation so stealthily that it took me off guard.

When I steadied myself, I realized the message was clear. Dominic liked me.

"Yes, I would like that too." He looked at me with his hazel eyes. My cheeks were blushing as red as roses.

"We can start now with the basics," I suggested. "Tell me about your family."

EIGHT

It was comforting to find out that Dominic was from a small Oregon town and raised by two loving parents. It was amazing to compare his childhood to mine. He grew up throwing rocks by the river, and I grew up running through red lights, so I didn't have to stop my watch on a run.

But as with everything in life, you meet people for different reasons, and I truly felt that Dominic was here for me. I saw his presence as comforting, and it felt easy to share my faith and my struggles with him.

After he drove me home from the airport, he asked me out to the burger place again. This time, I knew it was a date. A couple days later, I was cooking a meal for him—chicken and rice, of course.

Our boss finally figured out we liked each other and stopped scheduling our lifeguard shifts together. That didn't stop us from hanging out. It made us want to hang out more.

Before we knew it, we were on the green rugby lawn tucked away at the far end of campus. We had ridden our bicycles over with our yoga mats folded under our armpits. I wanted to have a stretch session outside. I called it a "stretch sesh." It was needed since training was ramping up. Dominic was just along for the ride.

Fall was in full bloom and the tri-colored trees of red, orange, and yellow brought color to life. I would say to my teammates that it was "unbe-leaf-able" as we ran under the trees on our campus loop. It was hard to watch them all go out and compete without me, but I was grateful to Dominic who also served as a distraction.

Our mats attached to all the lumps on the grass, making it impossible for a flat surface. It wasn't as ideal as I had imagined, but it was good enough. I had a light purple mat that reminded me of a unicorn. It was old and thin, but it still had some magic. Dominic had a sleek black one that was an inch thick, perfectly new since he bought it just for this occasion.

"I was thinking that I could be the instructor, and you can follow along like we are in a class," I suggested, giggling a little at the thought of it.

"Sure." Dominic got into the tree yoga pose as if we were on a mindfulness retreat.

"I guess we are in the advanced class," I joked. "Okay, now to start let's get into a runner's lunge with the right foot forward and left knee on the ground." I guided my body into the correct position effortlessly and turned to Dominic. He was struggling. It didn't look like he ever stretched in his life. His body was fighting to balance itself.

"You can take your hands to the ground to stabilize yourself, or you can keep your hands on your hips," I said in a soothing instructor-like voice. I watched him decide if he was up for the challenge. He went for the hips but then went for the ground.

Before I could give the instructions to switch to the other side, my phone buzzed. I reached into the side of my black and orange Oregon State backpack and stared at the screen. It was Mara. I looked over at Dominic.

"Hey, my sister is calling me. I am going to take it really quick." He nodded and I stepped aside to answer.

"Hello, my beautiful sister!" I chimed into the phone.

"Hey, Jem, I need to tell you something, but you can't freak out." Of course, when she said that, my heart began to race.

"Uh, what's going on? Is it about Mom?" Concern invaded my face, and my smile disappeared.

"Yeah. Mom is in the hospital right now. She is stabilized. Something was blocked up in her digestive system, but I think it's okay now." Her voice was calm. I knew she was calming for my sake, to protect me, just like Mom did.

My head began to spin, and my legs quivered with adrenaline. I began pacing back and forth. I was sad and scared at the same time, and I felt the need to curl in a ball and wrap a blanket over me.

"How long ago did this happen?" I asked. Dad contacted Mara first, which made sense because she was now the person who helped inform the family what's going on. Important information would funnel through Mara first and then to the rest of us. It had to be this way, or else Dad would be too overwhelmed.

"About two hours ago. I've been texting with Dad. Micah is with them too." Mara sounded mellow over the phone. If she had any nerves, she was concealing it well.

"How are you feeling about all of it?" There was a pause. I could feel that she had something to say but wasn't sure how to say it.

"I've been thinking about it, and I think I am going to take the next semester online and stay home. I feel like I need to be there."

"Mom would love that so much. You are so good at taking care of her." I supported her decision one hundred percent. It made me want to do that too. But also, Mom would get better. I reassured myself. Maybe this is just a setback for a comeback? I rationalized.

"December is right around the corner, so it will be good to all be with her. I'm sure this was just a small setback. The doctors will have a perfect treatment in no time." My legs felt less jittery after saying that out loud. "It will be okay." I was reassuring us both.

When I got off the phone, I wandered back to my purple mat. Dominic had given up stretching and was cloud watching. He was lying on his back. When he heard my footsteps, he sat up.

"How's your sister?"

"My sister is fine, but my mom isn't. Well, she wasn't, but now she's okay. There was something wrong with her digestive tract, and I don't know the details, but she went to the hospital, and she's still there." I longed to give her a hug.

"I'm sorry, Jem. Is there anything you need?" Dominic stood up and stood right in front of me.

"Yeah, I could use a hug." We embraced in a gentle hug, his arms around my backbone and mine around his waist. I felt grounded at that moment, and I heard the birds chirp as they flew over us.

"I also need to go pray," I admitted as I pulled out of the hug. "I'm going to bike over to the chapel on Monroe Street. It's behind the Newman Center."

"Can I come?" Dominic raised his eyebrows.

"Yeah, if you want." I didn't want to force him to go with me, but I didn't want to deny him a chance to pray either. He nodded, and I proceeded to roll up my yoga mat.

Praying was the only thing I could do to help Mom. I wanted to get to the chapel as soon as possible. Dominic sensed my urgency, so he rolled up his mat with speed.

Once we locked up our bikes near the chapel entrance, I decided to give Dominic the lowdown of the place.

"Many students come in here to pray, and everybody prays silently. Some students kneel, and some sit, so you can decide which position works best for you. I do a combination of both. You will also see me genuflecting at the tabernacle because Jesus is present. There are Bibles in the back if you'd like to use one to pray with." I paused, reflecting if I missed anything. "Oh, and the bathrooms are in the entryway before the chapel door."

Instead of looking scared, Dominic looked intrigued. He seemed eager to pray in this space. We set our yoga mats on top of the white cubbies. I peered through the glass chapel door and spotted Sarah.

Before we went in, I scribbled, "please say a prayer for my mom" on a sticky note. I handed it to Sarah on our way in before

I genuflected at the tabernacle and took my usual spot in the right section, second row, second seat in.

Dominic followed my lead and kneeled right next to me. Instantly, I felt more at peace, safe in this prayer space where I could truly focus on Jesus.

As my eyes fixed on the tabernacle and the stainless-steel sunset behind it, I prayed that God would heal my mom. I prayed he would give her peace, and I prayed she would feel loved.

Twenty minutes later, I went from kneeling to sitting. I didn't have anything left to say, so I sat to wait if Jesus had anything to say to me. Dominic was already sitting, and I wondered what was going on in his head.

After five minutes of silent reflection, I felt a wave of peace ascend upon me. It was the power of the Holy Spirit, a divine force I had come to understand, that bestowed this solace. This sacred comfort also kindled a deep sense of hope within me. I placed my trust in God, believing that everything would turn out alright. I took steady, deep breaths.

When we exited the chapel, I asked, "How did you like it?"

"It was nice." I stopped walking and turned to face him. I wanted a little more explanation than that.

"Nice as in what?" I inquired.

"I felt very peaceful. It was nice to be quiet." I understood that the chapel was a unique place to pray with limited distractions.

"It's my favorite place in Corvallis!" I beamed, realizing its importance to me.

"I prayed for your mom in there. I really hope she gets better."

"Thank you, Dominic. Prayers are the greatest gifts." I locked my eyes on him and held them there, so he knew how serious I was. When it got intense, I looked away.

"I think I need some time alone to rest and recharge." I scratched my shoulder because it now felt itchy. It also gave me something to do as I waited for a response.

"Yeah, Jem, whatever you need. Can I come by later?" I had to blink twice to make sure that his puppy dog eyes were real. He was truly concerned about me.

"Yes, you can come over later. I'll text you."

We hugged goodbye, and I got a breath of his ocean scent deodorant. Then I went left, and he went right. The parting of ways felt dismal. Maybe because I was already a little sad, or maybe it was because I felt closer to him. Showing him, the beauty of prayer was something special that I am glad he accepted. So maybe, I was feeling happy-sad.

I'll leave it at that.

NINE

The next day I called Mom in the hope of being a shining ray of light over the phone. Mara had texted me she was discharged from the hospital and was back home. I needed to bring her spirits up if they were down. Little did I know that she was more than down.

"This cancer is not going away, and I'm deteriorating! I feel horrible, and I just want to sleep," Mom cried in agony over Facetime. Her face looked drained, and there was no color.

"Ah, Mom," I sympathized. "I can't imagine how you are feeling. Just keep persevering. You can do it." I was aiming to be encouraging, but my words felt cheesy.

"When I was at the doctors, I had a bowel obstruction, which is very abnormal. They ran tests and said my cancer count was at an all-time high." She delivered the depressing news in a despairing voice. "If chemo worked, it only worked for a little. The cancer is back."

I didn't know it was possible. She was doing so well. She had her mistletoe shot, and she gave up sweets, and she took all her medicine—all the vitamins she could have ever needed. And the juicer, that thing provided her with fresh nutrients. I didn't want to believe it.

"What if the numbers were off?" They must have messed up somehow. "What if it was a misdiagnosis?" Machines break all the time. There are mistakes.

"The numbers weren't off." The discouraged tone in my mother's voice sent me pacing across my room. I paced to the balcony, then back inside. I didn't want Sarah to hear my conversation.

"I'm also in a wheelchair for the time being," Mom said as she shuddered.

"A wheelchair?!" I didn't mean to raise my voice, but I couldn't conceal my shock.

"Yes. I don't like that I have to use it either, but I need it."

"Oh, Mom. I am so sorry." I suddenly felt trapped behind the phone. The ability to comfort her felt impossible right now. I needed to be next to her.

Being in another state away from Mom was difficult enough in general, but now with her health, it was almost debilitating. We hung up the phone shortly after because she needed to take a nap.

In my room alone, I stood frozen with my gaze locked in front of me unsure of what to do. I sighed long and hard, paving the way for my sobs that were to follow. As hopeless as my body felt, my mind wasn't ready to give in. There had to be hope. A cancer comeback didn't mean it would win, right? I didn't really know, so I avoided googling it.

Weeks after the trip to the ER, pain started to strike harder than ever. There was more discomfort than my mom has ever felt before—a sensation Mom described as a set of knives jabbing in her rectal area and through her stomach.

There seemed to not be enough cushions to ease her pain. Dad would use three pillows to maximize comfort, but even then, she rarely wanted a wheelchair push.

Our phone calls became depressing, and I found no hope in her voice. Mom's mental state started deteriorating as rapidly as her body. I discovered Mom was shrinking in size and was having trouble eating again.

Angry and frustrated from the pain, Mom would swear under her breath in a harsh tone of voice. It felt difficult to hear her voice over the phone. After each phone call, I ran hard, yearning to run every bad thing away from my mom, desperate to make all the pain, physical and mental, disappear.

I was sad for my mom, yet quite terrified for her. I was merely watching the gradual deterioration of my mom's life, but my mom . . . she was the one living it. How can one's mind process the thought of death?

As the pain intensified over the days, my mom's attitude toward cancer grew increasingly bitter. She would curse, cry, and allow herself to vent her frustrations until she had emptied all her emotions. It felt as though the cancer was not only ravaging her body but also eroding the very cells responsible for her happiness.

For a week when we Facetimed, I could see the distress in her eyes. Her eyes would tremble in their sockets, and her frown mark between her eyebrows sank into her skin. Her cheeks were thin, making it obvious that she had lost even more weight.

They say without suffering, nothing is transformed. I wondered if transforming could be a bad thing. Could my mom be transformed into a miserable human being? It couldn't be. I knew she was stronger than her illness. I had to have hope.

I prayed without hesitation, longing for peace to flood Mom's body and soul. I prayed for the outpouring of strength from within her tiny body and for the Lord to make her full of life again.

Then came the call of despair. It was only a month after the ER scare.

"I want to get the pills." There was a strong confidence in her voice. She was outside on the backyard patio, and I was sitting on my bed in my fuzzy baby blue bathrobe. I watched her get infuriated with the small task of moving another cushion against her back.

"What do you mean pills? You have all the pills you could want." A sense of unease seeped into my core.

"Jem, I want to die. I can't live with this pain anymore." The sentence hit me like a punch in the chest. Shock flowed through my body, but it was anger that overtook me.

"No, Mom; you are not going to get pills that make you die." Instantly, tears streamed down my face. The thought of her taking her own life was tragic. But it was also selfish. I couldn't lose her.

This was not going to happen on my watch. I was looking back at her through the screen with full seriousness in my expression and tone. "You can't."

"It's my decision, and I'll take them if I want to take them." She mirrored the same tone of seriousness in her voice. I studied her famished face and searched for a semblance of hope. All I saw in her features was desperation. She was desperate to end her pain.

"No, you can't," I answered as sternly as I had before. I felt as if I was telling a child they couldn't get a Band-Aid after they cut themselves. The only solution to healing seemed lost.

"You don't have a say in the matter," she responded.

"MOM, YOU CANNOT KILL YOURSELF!" I yelled. I was standing up now and wanting to have a tantrum like a three-year-old. I was enraged at what she was saying to me. It was unimaginable that she would even think about taking her own life. I took a deep breath and tried to explain myself.

"Mom, you can't take your own life. It's such a gift. It's a gift to me and to the whole family and to your friends and to random strangers! God gave you this life, and you can't end it when you want to. God's timing is perfect." I tasted the saltiness of my tears as they drained into my mouth.

"I don't have the pills now. I have to make some phone calls and talk to some doctors, but I will let you know what I decide. Nothing is final." I could sense that she was trying to calm me down and end the conversation at the same time. It was hard for her to say this, let alone hear my reaction. But that didn't make it right. It wasn't right.

When I hung up, my mind was on blast, working to cope with what was just said. I quickly laced up my sneakers to go on a run. My phone buzzed, and I jumped hoping it was Mom calling me back and changing her mind.

It was Dominic. I was not in the mood to feel like talking, so I tossed it on my bed and let the door slam shut behind me. This was going to be a long run.

For a whole hour, I fumed. I released my anger through the streets of Corvallis. I was on edge, which only made me sprint harder. It was my day off, but I didn't care anymore. I was going to run until I couldn't run anymore.

On mile seven, I looped around and ran toward the chapel on Monroe Street. I needed to speak to Jesus. Completely sweaty, I used my black Nike shirt to wipe my face. Then I marched into the chapel with one mission, to pray for Mom.

Nobody was in there, so I decided to pray out loud. The light beamed through the blue stained-glass window on the side wall creating a rainbow glow along the chapel floor. I admired the colors and took a deep breath. The way light created colors still amazed me.

I fixed my eyes on the gold tabernacle. It was just me and Jesus.

"Jesus, I just feel so horrible right now. My mom wants to die. She can't die. Please help her not take these pills. Please. Show her Your love. Be with her, please."

I bowed my head and admired the rainbow once again. Something inside me understood that He was listening. I stayed silent and let my heart open.

After what I perceived to be quite some time, I ended my prayer. The sweat from my run was making me chilly. It was time for me to shower.

I was heading back to Monroe Street when I saw Dominic coming out of the Newman center. I avoided going in there because I was a sweaty mess, and I didn't feel like seeing anyone. I guess my plan failed because here I was in front of Dominic.

"Hey, Jem, I tried calling you. I wanted to see how you are doing." He looked at me with kindness, and I felt seen.

"Well, I've been having a bad day. I just need some time alone." I wondered if he could see the residue of my tears.

"We can talk about it . . . if you'd like. I'm here for you." I could barely accept his sweetness because my emotions were so out of whack.

"My mom's not doing well, and I just don't want to talk about it. Not right now." I felt on the verge of tears, and I wanted to wait until I was alone to release them.

"Oh, Jem, I am so sorry." He opened his arms for a hug. The warmth of his hug made my shiver bumps go away.

"That's why I was here actually. I wanted to talk to John about why God doesn't answer our prayers."

"What do you mean God doesn't answer our prayers?" I got defensive.

"Well, I know that you've been praying for your mom a lot and that God hasn't healed her, and I don't see why He can't just heal your mom." His voice seemed more quiet, afraid of how I might react.

"God doesn't always work like that," I declared. "You have to have faith that He will work the way He needs to work for His good plan. You have to trust that He is good."

"That doesn't make any sense," he answered, still calm.

"God doesn't always make sense, but you have to trust that He loves you. I know He does. God loves me, He loves you, and He loves my mom so much. His love is unsurmountable!" I yelled not knowing why. "I mean He created us! We wouldn't exist without Him. And we wouldn't have known each other without Him." My head was spinning, and I didn't feel like going into a theology talk with him. I didn't want to be questioned, and I didn't want to argue. I just wanted to cry.

Dominic could tell my heart was hurting aside from the discussion we were having. He reached over and touched my left shoulder.

"I believe that God loves you, and I love . . . I mean I am sorry if I made you upset. I am just trying to learn about all this stuff. It's all new to me. Can I swing by later, and we can talk about your mom?"

I nodded my head yes. Sure, he could come over. But I needed to leave now. I was on the verge of tears, and I needed to face them alone.

I slowly backed away, and he gave me a wave, his hazel eyes dazzling with concern. I imagined my eyes looking like a sad child. I turned away and sprinted down the street in the direction of my house.

The minute I was out of sight of Dominic, I stopped to catch my breath. It seemed necessary that I should run as fast as I could, but now it seemed pointless. I ended up walking the long five minutes of what was left of the trek.

Upon reaching my house, a wave of relief poured over me. Privacy was here. I slammed the door behind me and headed straight for the shower. I turned the knob to the hottest setting and stayed there until I couldn't feel my face. I cried as I let the heat make me numb.

After my shower, I lay on my bed, belly side up and stared at the wall in silence. I didn't feel like doing anything.

"Hey, Jem! Dominic is here!" An echoing of Sarah's voice boomed through my bedroom door. It had been two hours since I knew where my phone was. Dominic must have texted telling me he was on his way.

As quickly as I could, I stripped out of my bathrobe and put on my gray sweatpants and black hoodie. I pranced to the front door, so I wouldn't keep him waiting.

"Hey, Dominic, come in." He didn't have to stop by now, but here he was.

"Would you like something to eat?" I asked knowing I had leftovers in the fridge.

"Yeah, sure. I'll eat something." He followed me to the kitchen.

"I have some leftover chicken and rice with broccoli if you want." I took the container out of the fridge and grabbed the salt.

"You always make the best food," Dominic declared.

"My brother would say otherwise." I placed the saltshaker next to his portion of food. We were in the nook, and the sun was already setting. Fall was making its mark.

Dominic munched on his food while we had small talk. It was odd to talk about the nothingness in the world when my world felt like it was crumbling down.

As Dominic explained his tactic of not being called on in one of his business classes, I peered out the window to discover that a bud of a single pink rose was coming from the bare bush. It was defying the season of fall.

"What are you looking at?" he asked as he stopped sharing his story.

"Oh, sorry. I was listening. I was just looking out there at that rose bud. It's all by itself, but it looks like it's going to bloom." It was fascinating.

"I like it. It's pink." From his answer, he didn't seem as interested. I turned my attention back to Dominic to continue our previous conversation.

"It's like you," he stated.

"What do you mean it's like me? Because I was wearing pink earlier today?" I asked.

"No." He shook his head. "I mean it's like you because you're trying to bloom too."

I didn't really understand. "I'm trying to bloom into what?"

"Well," he explained, "you're going through a hard time with your mom. While all this is going on you're just trying to bloom and be happy."

I pondered that thought for a second. "I see that. I guess I am just a struggling flower trying to survive." I glanced back at the pink rose, acknowledging our similarities.

Later that evening, I finally told Dominic about my mom wanting to take the pills to die. It was challenging for me to be vulnerable, but since I was a bud trying to bloom, I thought it was essential that I let some hard things off my chest.

"She can't do it." I shook my head. It was still unbelievable. Dominic inched closer to me and squeezed me. Even on my worst days, having Dominic by my side made me feel secure, allowing me to simply exist without the need to mask my true feelings.

"Maybe she won't. Maybe she will decide against it." I looked up at him. It was possible.

"I really hope so," I agreed. There was nothing more to say. I rested my head on his shoulder and closed my eyes. I suddenly felt sleepy.

We said goodnight and parted ways. As I lay in bed that night, sleep eluded me. My mind was wide awake. How could I drift off when a tidal wave of fear was crashing over me?

How's Mom doing? I texted Dad. It was ten o'clock. He responded quickly.

She's doing her best. I didn't really know how to interpret this message.

I kept my phone out to send another message, this time to Mara and Micah.

Keep praying for Mom, I texted.

Mara sent a red heart emoji with *"I am,"* and Micah sent a thumbs-up emoji. I never knew if Micah ever prayed, but if he did, just this one time, I would be grateful. If Mom wanted those death pills, it must mean she was in deep misery. Though pain is never wanted, killing oneself was a whole other matter of loss. I wasn't going to be the one watching her take her own life. That was on God's time.

I lifted my head up to the ceiling and prayed to the one who knew me best.

"God, please be with my mom and ease her pain. Help her remember that you are in control and that she doesn't need to worry. Please watch over her." I was still lying on my bed, too tired to pray on my knees.

I knew I had to trust God with my prayers. The mysterious power of God will always be unknown and misunderstood. The simple idea of pain and God seem to never go in the same sentence. I believe that pain exists even when God is present. I believe that pain was not caused by God, something that many people couldn't.

I didn't have all the answers, but I knew God had them all. I wish He could give me some of them. I wish He could give me peace. For some reason, I didn't have any. I felt restless and scared and deeply saddened by Mom's situation.

I don't remember how, but I soon dozed off without a thought of anything more.

The next morning, I woke up with a pounding headache, and I couldn't seem to understand where it came from. It wasn't from drinking because I didn't drink. It wasn't from too much sugar because I didn't even eat my daily dose of chocolate yesterday. It was from stress.

I stepped out of bed and immediately put my hand to my lower back. It was sore. Another restless night. After two in the morning, I couldn't fall back asleep. I tossed and turned the rest of the night. Why is it always at night when things are the worst?

As I inched my way toward the bathroom, I stumbled over my phone abandoned in the center of my bedroom. The collision sent a sharp pain shooting through my big toe. As I bent down to inspect the damage, my equilibrium betrayed me, and I tumbled to the floor, crashing into my dresser and striking my head. I curled into a ball and moaned. *Good morning to me.*

That mess of a morning dictated the rest of my day. I saw everything in a negative light. The minute I finished my oatmeal, I wished I had eaten eggs. When I didn't bring a jacket on my walk, I was cold. When I went to class, I was called on randomly. When I asked Dominic to hang out, he was working. It was just a bad day.

As soon as it turned five o'clock, I smiled to myself. *Only five more hours until bedtime.* I considered doing homework, but I ended up making dinner and then went on a cleaning spree. I cleaned the kitchen, my bedroom, and the bathroom all while listening to loud angsty music.

Cleaning gave me a sense of liberation and clarity. It was satisfying to accomplish something, and it filled me with pride. I recalled my friend Kaitlyn mentioning that tidying your space can also cleanse your soul, a sentiment famously attributed to Mother Teresa. I couldn't agree more. My soul felt fresh.

When I finally finished, I collapsed onto my bed, exhausted both mentally and physically. I longed to be alone with my sadness, yet I also craved the comfort of someone's presence. It was a tug-of-war between these conflicting desires until the decision was made for me. There was a knock at the door.

I opened the door to Dominic holding a basket filled with pharmacy drugs. I wanted to laugh and cry at the same time.

"I brought you some pain meds to help with any pain you have. I wasn't sure what you needed exactly so I bought everything."

I peered in the basket, and he really did have everything from ibuprofen to Tums. My eye spotted a bar of chocolate. He had everything covered.

"Where did you get this nice basket?" It looked perfect for a picnic.

"My mom gave me some rolls last time she visited. I thought you might like it." He handed it over to me. I let Dominic inside and set the basket on the kitchen counter.

"Well, I'd gladly watch over this basket until your mom visits again." I admired the basket more than the pills. But I needed a pill for my head, so I tilted my head back and dried swallowed one ibuprofen.

"If you need more, I'd be happy to get you more," Dominic assured me. I gazed at the basket of pills and then back at him.

"If I need more pills, it means I need to go to the hospital," I joked.

The joke only lasted a second and then I was in reality, understanding the severity of Mom's condition and not knowing what to go about it.

Dominic sat beside me and rubbed my back until it was time for bed, which meant I was alone with all my thoughts in the darkest part of the night.

TEN

A couple weeks trickled by like a slow stream in a narrow canyon. It was almost December, and the Oregon rain was coming on strong. It gave me a dreary feeling, and I missed the sunshine on my face. But I missed my mom more.

As fast as the raindrops hit my window, the mass of Mom's body was melting away. Mara flew home earlier and was giving me updates on how she was doing. However, despite Mom's body deteriorating, her attitude was getting better.

"You know, Jem, I've been thinking," Mom said on Facetime as she lowered the stack of cards to the coffee table in front of her. She was in the middle of a solitaire game when I called her.

"I am not going to take the pills." Instant relief soothed all parts of my body. Muscles I didn't even know were tense, were released. My heartbeat slower, and I finally felt comfortable in my chair. I was proud of her for making the right decision and thankful to God if he had a part in that.

"I am so glad to hear that. Thank you. You were scaring me when you wanted them," I replied honestly.

"But I did decide one thing. I am not going to do the next round of chemo. It's not working anymore, and I am sick of the draining sensation and the hair loss and the chemicals. It's not worth it."

"You're just going to rely on the mistletoe shots?" I asked, hoping she was going to do something.

"Yeah, I will still do that but at this point, it doesn't really matter anymore. The cancer is winning, and I will die a natural death whenever I'm ready." Despite the bleak news, her tone remained resolute, leaving me puzzled.

Her words rattled me. She couldn't actually be dying. I wanted her to die a natural death, but I didn't want it to happen now; I wanted it to be in fifty years! Once again, I found myself rising from my chair and pacing around my room.

Struggling to breathe in the thinning air, my voice turned raspy as I cried out, "This can't be happening to you. You can't die." My words carried a forceful urgency, as if they held the ability to heal her illness.

"Oh, honey, it's happening. I was just at the doctors, and they said it's not looking good. There is nothing more they can do. Even chemo won't stop cancer from spreading. It's increased significantly, too much to stop." At last, I detected a hint of worry in her tone, particularly aimed at me, given my evident distress.

"I'm coming home." I had already pulled my laptop out of my backpack to search for plane tickets.

"Yes, please, Jem, I would love that."

* * *

It was easy to navigate the airport when flying on a random Tuesday morning. Dominic had offered to drive me, but the ride was stiff and unpleasant because my mind was occupied with other things. I felt myself pushing him away. I was overwhelmed with worry, and I couldn't handle sharing my heart with someone when my heart wasn't fully there.

"Jem, I know you are going through a lot right now." Dominic spoke through the thick silence in the air. He glanced at me to make sure I was listening. "You can let me in."

Rage surged within me, catching me off guard; I hadn't even realized it was simmering beneath the surface. Lately, stress has been dictating my emotions, leaving me unable to think clearly.

"I don't know what to tell you because I don't even know what we are!" I felt the heat in my chest, and I stopped myself for a moment before speaking again.

"I am confused by the relationship, and I am confused how my mom is getting worse, and I am confused how to handle it all, and I just don't know!" I wanted to bury my head in a blanket, but in the car, I had nothing, so I looked out the window.

We rode in silence for quite some time. Dominic gave me space and let the motion of the car relax me.

"I am sorry, Jem. I haven't been clear with you, and I'm sorry you're going through so much. But there is something that's been on my mind a lot. Can I ask you a question?"

"Yes?" I was lured in by what he wanted and intrigued with what he could be thinking about me.

"Will you be my girlfriend?" Suddenly, my nerves danced, and my anger dissipated. I wanted to twirl with delight.

"Yes, of course!" The giddiness of my voice echoed in his Jeep Cherokee. I leaned over his seat and gave him a small kiss on the cheek, and I flashed him a smile.

"I just won't be able to call you consistently because of my situation," I stated. I wanted to make sure it was clear that Mom came first. Dominic chuckled.

"What are you laughing at?" I asked.

"You don't need to change anything. I know you are going through a lot, and I will not expect a call from you. If you call me that's great; but if you need to be with your mom that's great too. Your mom needs you."

For the first time that day, my heart felt full of love, and I was eager to share some of it with Mom.

Dad picked me up in the loading zone without any stress. There was no traffic, and driving home was a breeze.

When we parked in the driveway, I scanned him for a moment. Dad was thinner than when I last saw him, his jeans baggier than before. Thick bags protruded from under his eyes, and there was an aura of coldness engraved on his shoulders.

"Thanks for picking me up; I appreciate it," I said as I unbuckled my seatbelt and tried not to stare at his new appearance.

"Of course, Champ." Just then I saw a hint of glimmer in his eyes, a sense of happiness. He was happy that I was here even amidst the worry he felt.

"How are you?" the robot in me asked.

"Jem, I am glad you are here. Your mom isn't doing well, and she is really excited to see you." Dad deflected my question to avoid his heart breaking even further. The love of his life was dying. What could be worse than that?

"I'm excited to see her too," I said, preserving Dad's feelings. Then in silent agreement, we headed up the driveway.

Mom opened the front door before I even had a chance to knock. We immediately threw our arms around each other in a tight embrace. I could feel every contour of her backbone against my fingers, and her bony shoulder blades pressed into my chin. When we finally pulled apart, I took a good look at her and saw how emaciated she had become.

I was initially overjoyed to see her, but now, a sense of fear gripped me. Her face appeared gaunt, with prominent cheekbones jutting out from her skin. Her wrists were as slender as a child's. Despite any attempts with clothing, makeup, or wigs, it was impossible to conceal the fact that she was unwell.

"You're so skinny!" I said, my concern slipping out.

"Yes, I know. I hate it, but I can't help it." Her voice held a hint of annoyance. "So come, tell me everything," she coaxed, changing the topic.

I let the topic slide. It was out of her control, and I felt bad for making it known. She eyed the green couch, and I followed suit.

"Well, there's nothing much to tell," I stated. "Running is okay, and school is going fine." I wasn't going to tell her that I was so worried sick about her it consumed my mind, and that rage and sadness fueled my runs and my missed practices.

"Welcome home, Jem," a voice called from the entrance of the room. It was Mara.

"Mara! You're here!" I ran up to give her one of my tight hugs.

"Yeah. I flew home right away," she whispered. "Got my finals done early and after Christmas, I'm doing my classes online. There is no way I can leave her looking like this." Mara momentarily widened her eyes, indicating her shared shock.

"I'm glad you're here," I said with normal volume. Mom didn't need to see us worried.

"I'm glad you girls are both here! I am excited to catch up and have girl time. But right now, I am feeling a bit sleepy. I might take a nap before dinner. How about you girls catch up?" Mom was already getting herself situated on the couch. Her demeanor was upbeat, which confused me. She was so different from a couple weeks ago; she appeared to be happy.

"Okay, sleep well." I walked over and kissed her forehead. Mara stood in the entryway watching, letting us share an intimate moment. I still couldn't believe how fragile she was.

"Let's go to your room," I suggested. We needed somewhere private to chat.

When the door shut, I let it all out in a loud whisper. "Mom looks scary! She is so skinny; she looks like she could die any minute. This is not good. Not good at all." I started pacing around the room seeing if I could rationalize the situation.

"Shh . . . keep your voice down, so Dad doesn't worry," Mara instructed.

"Oh my gosh, I forgot about Dad! How is he? Is he okay? He looks skinnier too, and he looks very stressed." I sat on the bed where Mara was sitting. Her bedspread was olive green, a color that matched the couch perfectly.

"He is not okay. He has worry drilled into his eyes! He paces around all day, and he is so distracted from work. His desk is within hearing distance of Mom's pains. He is eating less too, and it's just not good." Mara's forehead was creased, and I could see she was making a conscious effort to push the thoughts away.

"Well, what are we gunna do!?" I lamented.

"Shhh, don't let Dad hear you!" Her face got inches from mine. "We need to be strong for Mom. Like we discussed that day on our run." That day felt like years ago when it had only been five months.

"On the day we were going to see Mom after her surgery?" I acknowledged.

"Yes." Mara was standing now as if our discussion was over.

"Okay, I'll try to be strong," I concurred though I was not feeling as confident as I wanted to. "And remember we need to keep on praying. We can't stop. Especially not now." There couldn't be enough emphasis on prayer. If I could be confident, I could be confident in God.

"Of course, Jem, I will. You can pray extra hard since you like doing that." She gave me a nod as if it was now my job.

"Yes, I will." I was already planning on praying another Rosary after dinner.

"And Jem?" Mara continued to sound firm.

"Yes?" What else did she need to tell me, to not cry? I couldn't do that.

"Try to keep calm and not react so big." She displayed hand gestures as if I didn't know what big was. "Just be calm the best you can."

"Okay, yes, right. That makes sense." I nodded. I almost wanted to grab my pen and paper so I could write this all down.

"Yeah. We should probably help Dad with dinner tonight to give him a break," Mara suggested.

"Let's do it. I can make the chicken, and you can make the rice." I opened the door, and we headed to the kitchen, calm and composed.

At dinner, I wanted to bang my head against the wall. Mom had approximately two bites of her chicken. I counted. It took all my willpower to keep from grabbing her fork and feeding her. She needed to eat to survive.

"This is good, Jem and Mara, but I can't finish. I am so full." She caught me glaring at her plate.

"Sure, you can," I insisted, trying to sound more positive than pushy.

"No, I'm too full." She moaned, touching her stomach.

"How about a couple more bites." I was trying to find a midway point.

"I can't, Jem. The tumors inside me are pressing down on my stomach. I can't eat that much."

I returned her argument with silence. I wasn't going to force her after that. The image of tumors gave me a bad kind of shivers. I didn't even want to finish my meal. In comparison to Mom, I felt undeserving of food. *Why could I eat, and she couldn't?*

Dad and Mara waited in silence to see if I would get emotional. When I didn't, Mara broke the ice with her studies about accounting, a topic that can get Dad engaged. I tuned out the conversation while I finished my last forkful of rice.

When dinner was over, I followed Mom to the green couch. I took a seat next to her and felt my body indent itself into the cushion. It felt warm, and the lusciousness of the cushion pulled me in like a hug.

Sitting there next to her, I felt safe. The green couch had become a place of refuge. It was a spot of sadness and joy, perseverance and resting, pain and hope. When I looked at Mom, I felt sad, but I also had hope. This time my hope wasn't for healing; it was a hope for heaven.

"Mom, are you scared of dying?" I asked, finally bringing up the long-awaited topic. I wished with all my heart that she would say no.

"You know, Jem, I'm not. You have always been so good at reminding me of God's love and the future of Heaven. Your faith is very comforting. I am looking forward to seeing all my old relatives again." Her lips folded into a half smile.

"So, you've made peace with it?" I surveyed Mom's bony face and noticed it was completely relaxed, and she looked somewhat joyful.

"Yes, honey, I did. I am at peace with it." Her tone continued to display confidence. "I will look down on you from Heaven and watch you grow up."

"If you're not too busy chatting it up with Jesus!" I exclaimed as I wrapped my arms around my mom. I was so thankful she was in a state of peace and not in distress. It was good to know she was accepting of God's timeline and not her own.

Somehow, I had failed to understand that if she died, she would not be with me. I imagined heaven being an embrace of warmth, a place of welcoming and belonging. It was a place of joy.

But only Mom was going to Heaven. I was staying here on the earth without her. I couldn't bear to envision life without her; the thought was too heartbreaking. Instead, I chose to imagine her journeying somewhere free from pain, a trip of some sort.

"Speaking of Jesus, I have something for you." She reached across to the coffee table cluttered with about a dozen books on cancer research. Amidst them, there was a small box that had escaped my notice. Inside was a delicate gold chain, from which she withdrew a tiny gold cross. As she held it up to me, I noticed a circular emblem overlapping the cross, intricately carved with the image of Jesus and His Sacred Heart. The Sacred Heart symbolizes God's boundless love for humanity—a love that is selfless, merciful, and deeply passionate.

It was breathtaking, elegant yet deeply symbolic. It was a necklace that encapsulated everything I desired. A token of love and a piece of exquisite beauty. Mom gently placed the necklace in my hand. I held onto it, studying its details, running my fingers delicately over its surface.

"I thought you might like this. I was gifted it years ago, and I just found it when I was going through my jewelry."

"Wow, Mom, it's beautiful! I am going to put it on right now!" I clasped the necklace quickly around my neck. I admired it as it fell on my chest. The perfect resting place, right over my heart.

"I will wear this all the time, and I will think of you and Jesus. My two favorite people!" I leaned over and gave her a gentle side hug. Tears welled in her eyes, mirroring my own. At that moment, I vowed to wear the necklace every day.

"Oh, and by the way, I have some clothes to give you too," Mom added.

"We can go through them later. Right now, I just want to sit here with you." I needed to cherish this moment fully, knowing it wouldn't come again. There wouldn't be another like it. It was truly special, filled with faith and love, a memory I would carry forever.

We sat there for a while until it was time for Mom to take some medicine and stomach another bite of something. I didn't want to witness her struggle this time, so I headed to my room and checked my phone. I was curious if Dominic had texted me.

There was a text from Dominic. My emotions shifted quickly. Just seeing the notification of the text on my screen sent a giddiness up my stomach.

Hey, Jem, how was your day today? I am really missing you and your energy. I hope you are giving a lot of love to your mom.

I read the text over three times trying to savor the joy it brought me. Someone was checking in on me, missing me. It dawned on me then—throughout Mom's ordeal, we'd been checking in on her, but who would look after us once she couldn't anymore?

Dominic's message meant more to me than he would know. Dominic was making sure I was okay. He was in a way, filling a void that I didn't realize was there.

I replied. *Hey, Dominic! It has been hard and good at the same time. We have moments when we are talking deeply and connecting, and then there are moments when her sickness is getting the best of her, and it's hard to watch. Thank you for asking. How are you?*

I saw the three dots indicating he was typing back.

I am well. I just got home for winter break, so I am relaxing and eating my mom's good cooking. I tried praying, but it hasn't been going well.

I couldn't help but feel sad that my mom couldn't cook anymore. But that wouldn't be fair. I couldn't compare our situations. It would be no use. I took a deep breath and thought of the latter part of his text.

What do you mean praying hasn't been going well?

He typed back. *I try praying and nothing happens. I don't know what I am doing wrong.*

I sighed. People always think that praying involves feeling a certain way or hearing God's voice. Good feelings and sensing God's presence can happen, but they aren't guaranteed.

That's okay. Nothing has to happen. As long as you are lifting your heart to God, then He sees and hears you. Don't get discouraged! I am off to bed, and I hope you sleep well. :)

I slipped in a happy face to convey my lighthearted tone to him. Deep down, I missed him, though I hesitated to admit it outright. I longed for his company, his unwavering support. I found myself reminiscing about us in the car, the moment he asked me to be his girlfriend, and a smile crossed my face.

I had to think of this moment in order to fall asleep.

ELEVEN

"We're going to the beach today," Dad announced in front of the family.

Mara and I were preparing our oatmeal to fuel us for our run. Our morning routines had blended as they always did when we were back home. We would be eating by eight and running by ten. Micah had just woken up and was standing there half asleep. Our heads turned toward Dad.

"I was talking with your mom late last night, and she really wants to go to the beach one last time." Dad managed to say the sentence without choking up.

I refused to entertain the idea that she might only have one more chance to go to the beach. The thought of everything having a final moment felt depressing. Mara, reading my expression, spoke up.

"Mom wants to go at least one more time with the whole family. It will be good." Mara's tone was light and happy as if she were talking to a five-year-old, which we all knew was directed at me.

Mara placed her bowl of oats in the microwave while I stood there unaware that I had been mixing dry oats for the last two minutes.

"Okay, well, how are we going to take her in the wheelchair?" I asked, unsure of how this was going to work.

"We will figure it out. Mom really wants to go. You know how she loves the beach. It's her favorite place." The microwave beeped, and Mara pulled the bowl out and scooped a big blob of peanut butter on it.

"East Cliff Drive has a lookout with a parking lot. There is a short walk along the cliff, and it's paved." Dad was already thinking ahead, planning the perfect trip, or at least, a doable trip.

"Excellent!" I chimed in as I poured some almond milk on my oats. "Mom loves the sound of the ocean." I imagined the crashing of the waves on the beach shore and Mom being happy as ever. Mom had been listening to an ocean waves soundtrack on Spotify. She needed to hear the real waves and have a real adventure.

As we emerged from the silver Honda minivan, with its half broken right door and chipped paint on all sides, we were in a parking lot overlooking the sandy shore of Santa Cruz. The wind was mild and the sky blue, a pleasant evening for almost anyone to enjoy.

East Cliff Drive was the perfect place to park along the water. There was a little asphalt path that seemed suitable for a wheelchair.

When our request for a handicap permit was rejected, we were shocked. How could our sick Mom be denied the ability to get around? Dad threw out some choice words though he seldom swore. But he was right. It was totally unfair.

The more Mom felt ill, the more unfair life seemed for Dad. One thing after another led to Dad feeling angrier and less like himself. Not today, however; today was a beautiful afternoon, and we had found a parking spot. Dad was beaming.

"We lucked out!" he whooped as he pulled into the spot overlooking the water. The deep navy ocean blanketed the horizon, which contrasted with the light cobalt sky.

After three attempts to open the broken automatic door, the battery finally obeyed, and I slid out to receive the fresh salty air. I locked my eyes on the deep blue waves as I stood still capturing Mom's favorite view. The December sun felt warm on my skin, a simple kiss letting me know God was present.

I walked to the guardrails and leaned against them. I smelled the salty sea from a gust of wind. Micah stood next to me and took a deep breath.

"To think that we are in December, and it's this pretty," Micah commented, gazing into the mesmerizing horizon.

"I know," I agreed, taking the scenery in.

"We are fortunate to have lived this close to the beach all our lives." Micah had a point. We had enjoyed the beach on so many day trips. Rarely did we ever sit and appreciate how great of a gift that was. It seems that when dire moments occur, ordinary things become more special.

"I am grateful," I declared. Micah stared out into the waves lost in thought. I knew he was taking in the moment, letting it sink in before it was gone.

I could tell he was thinking about Mom; I could see a slight cringe in his face, a tenseness so small, only noticeable if you were close enough.

He took another deep breath, and I instinctively wrapped my arm around him. I rested my head on his shoulder.

"We really have to take it one day at a time, one moment at a time." What once was a clique saying was now words of wisdom. It was crucial to take it one day at a time, especially knowing there were only a few days left.

"Yes, we have to," Micah agreed. I could tell he was lost in thought again, and I was afraid he was getting too sad.

"Well, it's a perfect day just for Mom! Let's go wheel her around!" I grinned, desperate to shift the mood to excitement. We both turned around to attend to the others.

My sister, always on a mission, had already unfolded the wheelchair and assisted Mom in. Stacked high with cushions, there was no way Mom was going to be uncomfortable.

"I am so happy to be here! It has been so long!" Mom exclaimed. Her face was as bright as the sun.

"It's a beautiful day just for you, Mommy!" I suddenly felt like a seven-year-old, trying to make her mom happy.

"Let's walk along the path," Mara urged, the words stern but friendly. She guided the wheelchair to the left along the asphalt. My dad, brother, and I shuffled behind.

As we strolled along the cliff, I felt peace. I was almost positive that everyone else was feeling peaceful too. The blissfulness of the day was too overpowering to not affect you.

Two minutes into our slow stroll, Mom broke the peace.

"Oh, no!" Mom shouted. "Roll me to the bush!"

The urgency of her voice startled me, and I jumped up.

"What's wrong?!" I squealed and froze.

A hand pushed my left shoulder, and I stumbled to the right. It was Mara who now moved me out of the way so she could get near the bushes. Immediately, Mom bent her body sideways, my sister's hands now holding back Mom's hair as she regurgitated in the bushes. Then she let out a moan.

"Oh no, should we call 911?" I fretted. "Are you okay, Mom?" I went into emergency mode. My heart was racing.

"Jem, she's fine! She just needed to barf." Mara gave me the stink eye, clearly agitated.

"Here, Mom." Mara handed her a napkin to wipe her face. "Are you all done?" Her voice was calm and steady as if that whole scene didn't even happen.

"Thanks, Mara. I think I'm done." She handed the napkin back to Mara.

Blurred with a disturbing sight and a profound empathy toward my sick mom, I tried to shake it off. I suddenly felt sad, confused, and angry. Poor Mom had to be this sick. It wasn't easy to see her like this. Mom came here to enjoy the beach, not to be reminded that her condition was both gruesome and devastating. I lingered in the back of the pack, breathing deeply to steady myself.

I watched Mara and Mom's interaction. They were both so calm. But they had all the reasons to be. This was a normal occurrence. This happens every day now.

I wanted to be brave like my sister who seemed like a strong tower for Mom. It was just hard.

"Are you okay to keep going?" Mara asked gently in Mom's ear.

"Yes," she responded and nodded. "Heck, I have been waiting for this, and I want to stay." Mom was insistent, so we kept going.

"Here," Mara said to Micah, letting go of her grip on the wheelchair, giving him the opportunity to push Mom.

When we started walking again, Mara whispered to me, "Jem, remember to hide your fear. Mom doesn't need to see it. She doesn't need to see your worry."

"I'm sorry. I was shocked," I answered honestly.

"I know it's hard for you to help it, but if Mom needs to vomit or screams in pain, just step away, and I will handle it. I've seen it all."

Mara's eyes were soft but there was strength in them. She seemed as if she was going to cry but also run a marathon. It was a mixture of brokenness and intensity. Mara had witnessed so much of Mom's suffering, yet she fought through her emotions to care for her.

Mara was living up to her name. She was a true Martha from the Bible, fueling all her actions out of love. That's the way she had to love Mom, to be her caregiver. It was a sacrifice, an act of true love.

I wanted to express to Mara how grateful I was for her kindness, to shout it from the rooftops, to yell it across the ocean. Tears welled up in my eyes.

"Please, don't cry. Not now. Let Mom have a good day." Mara blinked and the sadness left her eyes, now fully filled with strength.

"Okay, yes." I sniffled and used my shirt to wipe the corners of my eyes.

"Come on, guys!" Micah shouted from a hundred yards away, still wheeling Mom down the path.

"Coming!" Mara yelled back. We both jogged toward them.

Mara's vulnerability struck me deeply. The sadness glimmering from her eyes was pungent, matching my own. She was heartbroken, and I knew that Micah and Dad felt the same way, hiding their pain just like us. We were all doing our best to stay strong for Mom. *How would we endure this?*

Soon, unexpected laughter erupted from the amusing situation we found ourselves in. The asphalt path led directly into the sand. It was completely impassable for Mom's wheelchair on such an uneven surface. There was a bench, but you had to march through the sand to get there.

"I'd like to go down to the beach," Mom urged.

"We can't roll you out there, hun," Dad logically explained.

"How about I just drag her to the bench?" Micah chuckled.

"Great idea!" chimed Mom. Micah was tough; it was easy for him to drag Mom across the sand. We all sat on the bench next to her.

"You guys go, and I can enjoy the view from here," Mom announced with perfect pleasantry in her words. She was totally fine to be left alone to appreciate the sensations of the beach.

"No, we're not leaving you." Dad was stern and protective.

"I'll be fine here. I'll just watch the water from here. Please go enjoy it." It was her day, so we let her have her way. We left her by the bench in a wheelchair alone.

Inches to the water, Micah started to giggle. "Look back at Mom. Doesn't she look funny? Who would leave a lady stranded on the beach in a wheelchair?"

We all looked back and started giggling. It was comical to say the least. It felt good to laugh. It was a short relief from stress.

We took a fifteen-minute walk along the shore in silence. We let the ocean breeze consume us, and we got lost in our own thoughts. It was nice as it could be due to the circumstances. When we got back, we found Mom chatting with a couple who had sat down on the bench beside her. They were enjoying their burritos and laughing at something Mom had said.

"Hey guys, how was the beach?" Mom chirped. We could tell she didn't miss us at all. She had made friends where she was. Another comical image: Mom making friends when she can't even go anywhere.

"Nice!" we all replied.

"I was thinking, why don't we get burritos too? They smell delicious."

"I know a spot. How about you give me all your orders, and I will go get them and bring them back?" Dad listened as we gave him our requests.

"You have a beautiful family," said the blonde stranger who was now in the middle of our conversation.

"Thanks," Mom beamed. We all stood there and smiled while Dad shuffled back to the car.

"We will let you be. Thanks for sharing your story. Good luck to you." I could see the genuine concern and sympathy in her expression—she truly meant what she said. The blonde woman hooked arms with her partner and walked off.

Eating the burritos and watching the waves was a tremendous experience. Mom was overjoyed with the scenery, and she ate four bites of Dad's burrito. I was so proud of her. I didn't want this day to end.

"Guess what?" Mom blurted.

"What?" we asked in unison, our mouths full of bits of food.

"I forgot to tell you guys my new mantra. It's *attitude, gratitude.*"

"I like that it rhymes." I put my hand on her shoulder. "I also like that it's doable. Anyone can become more thankful."

"Exactly. I can say 'attitude, gratitude' whenever I want to complain about being in pain or feeling down. There are so many things to be grateful for even when I have cancer. Like my family. I love you all so much." Her smile spread wide and looked even bigger on her shrunken face.

"Aww, Mom." I felt my heart lift to the sky. "I am so grateful for you!" I wrapped her in a side hug and pressed my cheek against hers.

"We love you, Mom," Mara added.

"You're the best," Micah concluded.

"Thank you for bringing me here." Mom's face beamed with color and for a moment I believed that her happiness could somehow heal her body.

We watched the sun set on the horizon, painting the sky with tangerine and peach colors. It was like the sky was lit up just for Mom. All I could think was *"attitude, gratitude."*

Soon enough, she felt nauseous again, and we wheeled her back to the minivan. The rest of the way home, Mom slept, being soothed as the Honda drove the thirty miles home on the winding freeway.

* * *

After that evening, I witnessed Mom continually practicing her *"attitude, gratitude"* mantra. I saw how it empowered her to combat every tickle of pain with the focus on the beauty and good around her. I saw her choose appreciation over frustration. I also saw her reading spiritual books over regular stories.

When Mom threw up, she was blessed she could still eat. When she couldn't sleep, she sat up with glee and read her book. And when she was stuck bedridden during the day, she called her friends. With her new devotion to *"attitude, gratitude,"* she saw the light in all things and embraced it as much as she could.

Her mantra allowed her to become aware of the quiet blessings in the day to keep her moving onto the next one. She needed to make her reality positive. It was inspiring.

TWELVE

Upon waking from my midday nap, I felt the afternoon light creep across my bed creating a beautiful glow. It seemed like God was present. I sat up and smiled. *Attitude, gratitude.* God was with me.

Twenty minutes later, I sauntered to the living room with the goal of sharing my joy with Mom. I could hear music as I approached, and I saw her lying on the green couch holding her phone.

I followed the tunes into the room. I could see the afternoon light shining elegantly through the biggest window in the room, kissing Mom's face. Another sign of God.

Her one dollar reading glasses were pressed against her nose, and I could see her squint at her phone trying to decipher the song title. She was flipping through her Spotify radio, listening to half a song, and adding it into her newly formed playlists. Her new stationary hobby was finding unfamiliar songs and organizing them into playlists depending on her mood. I think she had more fun sorting the songs than actually listening to them.

I bounded over to the right side of the couch leaning my hip on the armrest and peering over her shoulder. I interrupted her train of thought.

"Hi!" I exclaimed with a peppy spirit.

"Hi, honey," she answered, mirroring my tone but less high-pitched.

I crept beside her and put my face right next to hers. "Nice jams. Want me to dance for you?" I thought she could use some more entertainment.

"Sure, honey!" She put down her phone and turned toward me. I made my way to the dance floor, an unoccupied patch of carpet.

"Get it, DJ." I hummed and then I started dancing. I pranced around the room and let my body sway to the rhythm of the music. My arms went in all different directions. My legs shuffled, slid, and stomped.

Then I got really into it, and I shook my butt. I started laughing so hard I had to cross my legs so I wouldn't pee myself.

Mom was laughing too, but she encouraged me to go on. "I like the butt shaking. Now move your hips!" I did what I was told and let my hips sway to the beat. After twenty seconds, Mom changed the song, so I switched up my moves. Again, she'd switch, and I would change it up to match the beat. On one song, I launched myself into multiple twirls. I felt graceful and silly at the same time.

Then a slower song came in the queue, and I decided that it was a good transition to sit my butt on the couch and take a break. The slow song was soothing and actually very peaceful, a good song for a funeral.

"This sounds like a funeral song." The words came out of my mouth before I even realized what I said.

"You can play whatever song you want at my funeral," she said casually.

"Okay, sounds good," I uttered, realizing how odd it was to speak about her death. Mom caught on to that I was unsteady.

"God is good. His timing is perfect timing." A soft smile pressed up against her face.

"Yes, God is good," I agreed. I felt comforted that Mom trusted in God. Too bad God's timing wasn't our idea of perfect timing. I leaned in and gave her a hug making sure I was delicate. My poor Mom. I didn't want to let go.

The doorbell rang, and it jolted me. We had visitors.

"Oh, a bunch of my friends said they would stop and visit this week. I told them about any time before dinner, so here they are! Nice and early!" Even with her extreme fatigue, Mom's lack of energy turned into a bolt of lightning when her friends were here.

I marched over to the door to show some enthusiasm. In reality, I wasn't excited at all. I wanted to spend time with Mom. I didn't want her friends to come in. I had limited time with her. How dare they waste it.

"Hi! Welcome!" I greeted them with a big fake smile. "Come on in. Mom is right here." I gestured toward the open room where Mom transitioned from the couch into her recliner. It now looked like a throne with her small body drowning in it. She had selflessly given up the couch so her friends could sit comfortably.

I longed to join the conversation, but Mom needed alone time with her friends. She also was probably going to talk about cancer, which I didn't need to hear at the time. I headed to my room to pray with my blue Rosary and wait for them to leave.

When more people were getting the memo that Mom's cancer was not going away, more of her friends came to visit, and I was left retreating to my room in annoyance. Because Mom was such a ray of light, people longed to maximize their time with her. And for that particular reason, it angered me because I wanted more time with her too. I didn't want to share.

Mom's pale slim somber face brightened with shades of pink when her friends arrived at our doorstep. In one instance, Mom could be sullen eyed from a nap and the next instance, she was filled with fire as she sat up on her chair and faced her friends.

I tried to be as accommodating as I could and let her friends have their visit. When they departed, I would enter the room and salvage what was left of Mom's radiant energy.

In addition to the visits, her friends would bring baskets of gifts. When they left, Mom and I laughed. The presents were nice gestures, but they were totally useless for Mom. She didn't need anything. She was going to die soon.

I sauntered into the room after a group of her girlfriends had left our house; I was curious to know how the visit went. I saw she had a box of goodies. I huddled next to her to peek at what she received.

"Look!" she exclaimed, "more lotion!" We both bent over laughing. The amount of lotion she was given was insane, as if she cared about dry skin anymore.

"Hey at least you got some fuzzy socks!" I snickered, pulling the socks out of the gift box and holding them up. The pink sparkly socks looked like they were meant for a ten-year-old. We laughed some more and placed the box on the right side of her chair with all the other treasures.

"How was your time with the 'girls'?" I asked, interested in the quality of the visit.

"It was so fun, but now I'm so tired. I am going to need a nap. Also, some water. Honey, can you get me some water, please?" Dad had heard her request from the other room and had filled a glass of purified water and delivered it to her. After she quenched her thirst, she set the glass down on the table beside her chair and gazed back at me.

"Do you need anything else before you nap?" I asked. I peered around the room looking for anything that Mom would need. "You want to wear your fuzzy socks?" I giggled. I enjoyed this silliness.

"Not now," she smirked. Her speech was becoming slower, a clear sign of her growing drowsiness. "Thanks, honey, but I'm good. I just need to rest my eyes. . ." And with a blink of an eye, Mom drifted to sleep. Although her friends uplifted her, conversing with them left her feeling drained. It was a lot of energy to fight cancer while maintaining a social life. It was impressive.

I left Mom to rest with a sad heart. My time with Mom was creeping away, and I longed for more. *I needed more time.*

* * *

"Hey, how's it going?" I asked Dominic over the phone. He had asked me to call him when I was free.

"Hey, Jem! It's so good to hear from you! I'm having a good time relaxing at home and not doing homework. I am excited that Christmas is almost here, but I miss you."

I had completely forgotten about Christmas. It was only two days away. Our lives have become slower yet more on edge every day. Witnessing Mom's withering body didn't mesh well with the joy of the season. But Mom's attitude was hopeful and that made all the difference.

But when it came down to it, I was at war with joy in my heart. Sadness and dread were pulling on it, and it felt like my heart was being operated on. It was obvious Mom's death was getting closer; how were we going to live without her?

"Ah yes, Christmas," I answered. "We have been so preoccupied with other things, but I'm sure we will relax on Christmas day," I lied. I don't think anyone would be relaxed except Mom. She would be entering Heaven, but as for the rest of us, we'd be left without her in despair. There would be a hole. I didn't want to think about it.

"Are you holding up, okay?" He could tell that I was not my peppy self.

"I'm okay. Reality is scary. My mom is withering away. But her soul is still there; her spirit is alive, upbeat. It is amazing to see her happy when a month ago, she was depressed." I was grateful for her turnaround in perspective. "She has a mantra, 'attitude, gratitude.' It's beautiful to see this change." I paused, taking in the situation. It was very special to see her like this. Not all people go into death with smiles on their faces. It was almost unbelievable but still, I believed.

I continued my thoughts, "But her body is slowly fading. Cancer is killing her, and it's so hard to bear. I'm trying to shove the pain down and act normal, but it's hard and I feel alone. I need love from my mom, but she's ill. She can't give me everything like she used to." *Who was going to take care of me when she died? A girl needs her mother.* A release of tears watered my cheeks.

Dominic didn't respond right away. I didn't know what he was supposed to say. It was an impossible situation to be comforted in. The predicament was unavoidable.

"Oh, Jem, I cannot imagine what you are going through. But I do know this: you are so strong in your faith, and you have a big heart. You can be there for your mom. You were meant to be there for your mom, and your big heart shows that. Maybe the roles are reversed now. Your mom was there for you, and now it's time that you can be there for your mom." I never really thought about it like that.

When I finally told Mom that Dominic was my boyfriend, her smile fell off her face. She was ecstatic.

"I am so happy for you! I also knew he was into you from what you had told me! Your first boyfriend! It's exciting!" She couldn't jump up and down because she was too weak, but I leaned in so she could give me a hug.

"I'm happy too, and I am also happy that it is Christmas Eve! Would you like to go to Mass with me?" I had asked her previous Sundays, but she always declined because she was too tired.

"Yes. I would really like to go with you." Her response was genuine.

"Yippee!" I squealed. "I love you!" I gave her another hug.

What took Mara seconds to unload the wheelchair, it took me ten minutes. Luckily, we arrived early, and I got Mom situated before Mass started. I rolled her to the wheelchair- designated pew and sat down next to her. I could feel people's eyes on us, and I knew what they were thinking. *Poor lady, she looks too young to be in a wheelchair.* They were right.

Mom was also too young to die, but I wasn't going to go down that road. *God's plan, not my own.* I repeated silently to myself.

The mass was beautiful. We both cried. I knew we weren't crying at the angelic music, which was exquisite; we were crying because it was going to be the last Christmas Mass she'd ever attend.

After the service, a petite Vietnamese lady came up to Mom and me with sympathy in her eyes.

"Who are you with?" she asked me.

"This is my mom," I clarified, unsure if that was what she was wanting to know.

Her gaze went to Mom, and she bowed her head a little. "May God bless you." Then she turned and faced me. "And may God bless you too." Then, she was gone.

I turned to Mom. "I think God just blessed us through that stranger."

"Well, if that is the case, I'm loving it!" She smiled, and I could tell she was trying to remain positive. She needed this holiday to be special.

For dessert that evening, Mara made Mom's famous flourless chocolate cake, a cherished recipe in our family for special occasions. I had helped get out some of the ingredients, but it was Mara who whipped up everything perfectly.

"Yummy! This is so delish," Mom remarked as she scooped up a small piece of cake on her fork. The whole family was out on the patio with their small plates of cake in front of them.

"Thank you, Mara, for making this. It's perfect. It is so good to eat sweets again." Mom had quit her healthy diet since it would do nothing to help her live longer.

"Anything for you, Mom," she said, really meaning the words.

"This is totally amazing!" Mom declared again as she ate another bite, savoring it in her mouth.

I closed my eyes and tried to feel what Mom felt. She had nothing but her taste buds and the people she loved. I opened my eyes and searched around. Mom was happy. Mara felt accomplished that a small piece of her love was shown through the cake. Micah was there, a constant peaceful presence. Even Dad seemed to be lost in the moment, enjoying the cake and Mom's joy.

I took a bite of cake, and it was more than amazing. It was incredible. The chocolate was intense, but what brought the cake to life was the happiness it brought Mom. The joy elevated in Mom's mood became a shared joy among us all.

THIRTEEN

I lay awake one afternoon, trying to take a nap but failing to do so. My tiredness turned into tears as I fathomed the tragedy that was set before me. I was absolutely positive at this point that Mom was going to die, and I was absolutely not okay with that.

After Christmas, Mom's illness had taken a deep dive. Her pain increased all the more, and she moaned constantly. Mara would rush to her side and give her pills to calm her while Dad would pace around the kitchen hidden from the scene. Micah would stay in his room, and I would go pray the Rosary.

My prayers had changed. I used to pray for Mom to heal from cancer. Now, I prayed for her to die peacefully and go to Heaven. *Was that, okay? Was I giving up hope that she could be completely healed, or was I being realistic?* The thing about God is that he is beyond realistic. He could do anything. I believed that nothing was impossible for God. I hoped God could understand where I was coming from.

After I prayed with my bright blue Rosary, my face was blotched with tears, and I had red patches staining my cheeks. I was hit harder than normal. Mom wouldn't be here soon. *What are we going to do? What would our lives look like without Mom?* It was too devastating to wrap my head around.

I carried my body in Mom's direction, to the green couch. I was the opposite of numb. I was alive with feeling. My heart pounded with an impenetrable dread with each breath I breathed.

Making my way down the hallway, I spotted Mom standing up with a bend in her back so her tumor wouldn't be agitated. Our eyes met, and she saw my glossy eyes. Slowly she opened her arms wide and waited for me to gently embrace her.

"Jem, come here." She nudged me toward the couch. I helped her steady her stance as we sat down. Sinking into the enveloping cushion. This couch was our sanctuary, where our hearts lay bare and vulnerable. I couldn't do it anymore. I couldn't be strong.

"I don't want you to die," I sobbed as I buried my face in her shoulder, letting my despair flow out. This was the first time I really acknowledged my thoughts about her death.

Mom remained calm as if she knew exactly how I felt all along. She placed her hand on my back with tender care. She had an essence of peace about her. There was no pain in her eyes. It was hope. It was a pure beaming ray of hope that radiated— that created an aura around her.

"I know you don't. I didn't want to die either. Now, that I am going to die, I am going to accept it . . . surrender to it."

I imagined her surrendering herself in front of Jesus at the gates of Heaven. She would be happy in Heaven. But I would miss her too much. *How would I live without my mom?*

"You can't go. I need you," I cried putting my cheek on her shoulder, the only body part that didn't hurt her.

"The only person you need is Jesus. You taught me that."
She kissed my forehead. I did tell her that. Jesus is all you need.
Jesus is the hope.

"Honey, you are so beautiful. You are so loving and kind,
and you bring so much good to this world. I am so thankful you
are my daughter."

Such kind words were escaping my mother's mouth that
I was confused as to who was the one dying. Before I could
respond, Mom continued.

"I wanted to let you know that you are special and that I
love you so much. I also wanted to forgive you for anything
and everything you have ever done, and I would like to ask for
forgiveness for all the times I hurt you."

Failing to recall anytime Mom was indecent, I replied, "I
do, Mom. I forgive you. I love you so much. You are the best
Mom!" I looked her straight in the eye, but I couldn't hold it in.
"I don't want you to die!" I wailed. My words were hard to make
out with my sobbing. My heart felt like it was being beaten with
a metal rod.

"I will still be your mom. I will just be in a different
place." Her fingers grazed my back, and she laid her hand
on my shoulder. "What matters most is that you know I love
you and that I know you love me." She kissed the top of my
head.

"I do love you so much," I cried and wiped my tears with the
back of my hands.

"You know, Jem, I might be able to speak to you through
signs. And if I can, I will send you one." She kissed my forehead
again and let me cry. There were no more words to be said.

FOURTEEN

It was a bleak January afternoon, and Mom wanted to go outside. Recently, that was all she wanted to do. Unable to partake in meals, strolls, or even muster enough vigor for company, her world had shrunk to the confines of her sight.

We would position the wheelchair outdoors, allowing Mom to soak in the fresh air while she observed the world pass by. As I approached, her eyes, tired yet hopeful, met mine, mustering a feeble smile. I reluctantly slid open the glass door leading to the backyard. My gaze fell upon the uneven concrete, ensuring the wheelchair's stability in its designated spot.

Once I got the wheelchair in position, Dad and Mara lifted her down the two stairs and placed her down gently. I sprinted to Micah's room to tell him to join us. These afternoons became essential family moments.

What once was a thin and healthy five foot nine, 57-year-old, and 138-pound woman was now a fragile, emaciated 88-pound cancer patient. It was hard to look at her like that, her appearance reflecting the devastating truth of cancer. It could happen anytime now. God had the last say.

"What a blue sky today. We got lucky!" Mom marveled, observing the beauty of a world she might never see again.

I pulled out a patio chair for me to sit in that was near Mom. I gave her a smile as she admired the tree we had in our backyard for years. Micah sat down next and didn't say a word. I'm not sure if there was anything to say. Mara's face showed no emotion, but her eyes were dazed. Dad came out to join us but then paced into the house and back out again as if he had to keep checking the time.

It wasn't an exaggeration to say that we were all lost in despair. Fear and devastation and every emotion in between consumed us as we braced ourselves for the inevitable loss of Mom.

But amidst the heavy silence and the dreary atmosphere of our situation, Mom's voice, filled with childlike excitement, pierced through the air.

"Look, a hummingbird! Look, guys! Right there, look at it!" Right in front of Mom was this bright orange hummingbird playfully dancing before her. It was as if the hummingbird was saying hi to Mom, wanting her to be its friend. The beautiful bird fluttered for a minute, offering a fleeting moment of brightness before darting away.

"Wow, that was incredible!" Mom exclaimed, her eyes straining to follow the bird's flight path.

I stood up just to make sure I saw the scene correctly. The hummingbird was gone. I gazed off into the distance where it had come from.

I looked back at Mom. A genuine smile graced her frail features, and I found myself mirroring her expression. In that short encounter, that tiny creature had brought immeasurable joy to Mom's heart. It felt as though the hummingbird had chosen her, precisely when she needed it the most.

"That was the most beautiful hummingbird I've ever seen. Did you guys see that?!" she squealed.

"Yes, honey, we did," Dad said gently.

"Mm hmm," Micah said as he nodded.

"It's January, and there was a hummingbird! That was just amazing. That made my whole day!" The smile on Mom's face grew wider. "What a beautiful little bird."

In that bittersweet moment, I couldn't help but ponder the perfection of it all. Despite the looming shadow of death, Mom remained attuned to the simplest of pleasures, embracing each moment with the wonder of a child experiencing something new for the first time.

When you have cancer, life becomes about the small things. You don't really think about big plans or a long future ahead. Every day is just about getting through the day. Your world shrinks, but you start noticing the little things more, the small details around you.

Mom found happiness in those small moments. It was those little bursts of joy that kept her spirits up. She held onto them tightly, finding beauty in each one, especially when she saw that hummingbird flutter by. It was a special gift meant for her.

Her last happy moment was seeing that hummingbird. After that, she fluttered to Heaven.

PART 2

OVERCOMING THE GREATEST LOSS, THREE MONTHS LATER

FIFTEEN

Staring at the crucifix by my bedside, I flickered my eyelids trying my hardest to push back the tears in my sockets. So often I told myself I couldn't cry, but so often I lacked the strength to hold it back.

I studied the crucifix.

In silence, I compared my anguish to that of Jesus. I scrutinized the depiction—the nails piercing his flesh, the cruel crown of thorns encircling his brow, the thirst that wracked his body, his gaping wounds.

It was all so painful for Jesus. Just as it was all so painful here, lying in bed with what felt like a physical sensation of my heart being ripped out of my chest cage. I was in so much pain, yet I was still alive.

As silent tears fell effortlessly down my face and rounded my lips, I whispered to Jesus who I believed was somewhere in the room.

"Jesus, how did You do it? I can barely handle this pain," I moaned. I felt weighed down, my body anchored to the bed, unable to move.

Jesus's reply was silence.

He just did.

And so, will I.

For thirty minutes, I sat there wiping my tears away while more kept coming. The tissue box in my hand was my security blanket that I thought couldn't fail me. But sure enough, the tissues ran out.

* * *

After it happened, things were all off.

For a while, I didn't know what to think . . . if at all. I didn't really think. I was a zombie mindlessly following a constant daily routine as if everything was normal. I thought if my routine remained unchanged, then my life really wouldn't change either. *Right? Wrong.* I could barely function.

Ever since Mom passed, I hadn't been my full self. There were so many emotions raging within me. My body was heavy, and my mindset was dreary. Only a glimpse of the sun or a hug from Dominic could bring a smile to my face even if it was only for a moment. Most days, I was trapped in the sadness of grief that was impossible to escape.

Sometimes, I wanted to scream. Screams of sadness and anger would pound against my tongue, and I would have to hold it in before any words came out. If anyone around me started to talk about their moms, frustration would consume me—especially when they complained about their moms. I wanted to stand on a chair and yell with my fists raised, "At least you have a mom!"

I quit my lifeguarding job, and I wanted to quit the track team, but something told me I shouldn't. I loved running, and I enjoyed being able to set my mind free on runs.

Coach Lewis had generously let me continue training on my own. I had gone to practice once, and that was a disaster. I remember that day vividly. Tears were streaming down my face as I struggled through the mile mark on the track, overwhelmed by grief. I dropped to the ground and curled my body into a ball. I lay on the track making a big scene, but I couldn't stop crying. The grief was too much to bear.

It was better that I was alone. That I ran alone. That I ate alone. That I took my Saturdays alone. I would encourage Dominic to have a boys' night out and tell him that I was busy. I was busy being alone and sad.

Spring was here and instead of smiling in the mirror, I cringed at the droopy bags under my eyes, revealing my lack of sleep. I gently tapped the puffiness of my cheeks with my index finger, swollen from tears. I was disgusted that my reflection was afflicted with so much sorrow, a sorrow I couldn't hide.

I slipped into a short sleeve shirt and leggings, then drove myself out to the forest where one of my cherished trails lay hidden. This trail held a special place in my heart, as it was the very first one that I explored during my official visit to Oregon State.

As I pulled into the gravel parking space, it felt different than it once had. Today seemed darker, and the mist of the morning made it feel eerie and cold. I couldn't help but shiver as I tumbled out of my car and strolled toward the dirt entrance.

I did some jumping jacks and warm-up exercises to get my legs going. I started my watch and moved my legs up the first hill. I felt as if I was a horse pulling a carriage of bricks; my legs felt fatigued, and my deep breaths turned into giant huffs.

I knew it was going to be a hard run because I was already exhausted. That's all I ever was these days, sad and exhausted. However, I didn't think it was going to be this hard. But I told myself I couldn't quit. Running was the only thing I could do these days.

As I continued to run, my brain started to attack me. Nasty and hurtful thoughts spun in my head, critiquing my fitness and my future. *Jem, you are so slow. How are you a D1 athlete? How will you ever get back in shape at this rate? Outdoor track is already here. Will you ever be fast again? Will you ever race again? You could be forgotten.*

My self-esteem was becoming weak, and I had no mental ability to think straight. *Am I really that worthless?*

Right then, I yearned for the comfort of my mom. I wanted my mom to hold me and say that everything was going to be okay. I wanted her to whisper in my ear that she loved me. I wanted her to make a funny joke about something random to make me laugh. I wanted her to love me no matter how fast or slow I was. I needed my mom.

But she wasn't there.

Mom wasn't going to comfort me. She wasn't going to tell me that she loved me. She wasn't going to make me laugh. She wasn't going to fill the empty void I had in my heart. I needed her, but she wasn't here.

She was dead. And I was alone.

Tears began to stream down my face as my quads carried me up another hill. Once I reached the downhill, my quads could only shuffle. They were so tight. As I made my way down, I tried my best to see through the tears.

I drifted to the border of the trail and propped my hand against an enormous pine tree and cried. The short cries transformed into sobbing; my knees turned weak, and I was forced to squat down. My stomach began to churn, and my heart felt hollow. Nobody was around, and the forest was silent except for my cries. I was sad and alone.

The thought of being isolated in the forest completely vulnerable finally dawned on me. *I'm sad and helpless.* I searched around, and there were no people or animals in sight, and the mist was becoming more like fog. I felt more alone than I have ever felt in my life. It was horrible.

As soon as I managed to prop myself up again and return to a semi-normal breathing pattern, I walked back onto the trail. My legs were still weak, and my body shivered as my sweat became a coat of cold.

My body didn't want to move. I was cold, and I was tired and wanted more than ever to drape a blanket over me and have a cup of tea. I looked at my watch. I was at the halfway point. Whether I went forward or backward, I was just as far as I was close.

"Mom, I miss you so much," I said out loud, staring at the empty trail. "I wish you were here to give me a hug."

Dread dawned on me, but somewhere deep down, my faith emerged. *Jem, you can do this. God can give you strength.*

I used my hand to wipe away my remaining sniffles.

"God, please help me get through the rest of this run," I prayed to the sky. "I know You see me, and I know You hear me," I acknowledged. "Please run with me; be my strength. I have nothing left."

There was silence. For some reason, the silence was a response. I understood it as if God was saying, "Okay." I trotted forward to continue the loop, completely relying on God to get me back, trusting that my prayer was heard.

When I got home, I called Dominic.

"I'm tired of being alone," I told him. I felt vulnerable and exposed, but I felt safe.

"I will come over," he responded, his voice confident and caring.

"Yes, I want you here and I need you here. I just miss my mom so much, and I can't do it alone anymore. I can't," I cried. Crying was a normal occurrence for me. "I've been pushing you away, but I need you. I need somebody to love me. I need comfort." Exposing myself was a huge relief. I let myself be weak.

"I'm coming right over, and I will be with you as long as you need. I will care for you. I am here."

He came to me and stayed with me all day, our backs against the floor of my room, looking up at the ceiling. I reminisced about memories of Mom and let all the tears fall. Dominic was patient, and he asked questions about Mom, letting her memory stay alive.

"Do you want to know something cool?" I asked Dominic, sitting up from the floor.

"What?" He sat up and looked intently.

"Colette, my mom's name, well, it means people of victory in French. I think that's beautiful. I mean she wasn't victorious over cancer, but I think she was victorious despite cancer. I think she lived up to her name."

"I think she did too," Dominic replied and pulled me in for a hug. "She seemed like the best mama." He kissed the top of my head.

* * *

Today, I decided not to deepen my sad mood with negative self-talk about my dreary appearance. After that disaster in the woods, I needed to shield myself against anything that could deplete my mental energy. I avoided the mirror and walked toward the outside patio that was connected to my room.

The fresh Oregon air hit me like a wave of perfume. I breathed in deeply and let my eyes ponder the light pink rose bushes filled with life. *I wish I was filled with life.*

I watched the bugs on the pear tree crawl their way over the fruit. I got close to one and smashed it with my right thumb. Then I pulled a pear off the tree and threw it as hard as I could on the dirt below. My frustration was in full bloom.

It had been three months since I lost my mom, and everything felt out of place. The world didn't pause to grieve her; everything around me continued as if nothing had changed. I felt overwhelmed and unable to move forward, yet I knew I had no choice but to keep going. The thought of facing each day seemed utterly exhausting.

"Jesus, please get me through this day," I prayed. Though it sounded more like begging than a prayer, I knew Jesus wasn't going to mind. He knew I was sad.

Feeling a little wobbly, I sat on the patio chair and stared at the backyard with no motivation to get up. I felt my phone buzz.

I looked at the message and smiled. Finally, something good. It was from Dominic. He wished me good morning and asked if there was anything he could do for me. I texted back and told him I needed a hug. In actuality, I needed way more than one.

Within ten minutes, Dominic was at my door with his arms spread wide. I let my body float into his embrace and lingered there.

I finally let go, and my eyes started to water.

"I just miss her," I bawled, staring at his stomach instead of his eyes.

"I know you do, and that's okay. She was your mom." I slung my arms around his waist again and held on for another hug. He patted my back to soothe me, and it made me feel better.

"I also got you this." He pulled out a dark chocolate bar from his back jean pocket. It was the Endangered species brand, the tastiest dark chocolate ever, my all-time favorite.

"Just what I needed!" I exclaimed through my tears, lighting up from the gift. "Let's go eat it together on the patio." I grabbed his arm and pulled him in the house then out onto the patio where we ate chocolate and stared at the bugs on the pears.

SIXTEEN

My lungs felt frozen. It was hard to breathe. I was covered with sweat, and my covers had disappeared from my bed. I looked at the clock. It was 3:01 a.m. I walked to the kitchen and poured myself a glass of water.

The nightmares kept coming. I had witnessed Mom dying twenty different times now. My heart would break over and over, the absence of joy sucking me alive. People told me time would heal. I wanted time to speed up or end because it was hard to stay afloat.

I wasn't in the room when Mom had died, but in my nightmares, I was watching it all. It was terrifying and heartbreaking. I turned my thoughts toward Jesus to release me from the painful images.

"Please, Jesus. Be with me," I begged. "Please hold my mom safe. Please help her be happy and free of pain." I imagined Mom healthy and happy as ever, seeing all her relatives in Heaven, laughing with pure joy. It brought ease to my heart.

Until 3:30 a.m., I was fixated on the wall with no specific thoughts. In a daze, I hesitated to return to bed when I had a thought. I wandered over to my backpack and took out my blue Rosary from the side pocket. I slipped back into bed and placed the rosary beside my pillow. Then, I fell asleep. I didn't have any more nightmares the rest of the night.

Sarah handed me a cup of coffee the next morning; she had made an extra-large batch, caffeinated, just for me. She also pulled me in for a hug.

"How are you doing?" she asked. It was the usual question of the morning.

"How do I look?" I replied; my hair was in a deflated ponytail, and strands of hair were going in all different directions. I was still in my gray sweats and not planning on changing out of them.

"I think you need to get out of here. It might be good for you to go somewhere besides school, home, and church." She was drinking her decaf tea, and she placed her mug on the table. "Go, have some fun; have an adventure." She smiled at me.

I considered it. She was right. All I did when I got back to Oregon was cry, pray, and study. I was isolated from my friends and had failed to go to track practice. The coach had let me practice on my own, but that too, was becoming unhealthy.

"Yeah, you're probably right," I agreed. Sarah's eyes struck me. I couldn't help but smile at her even when all my joy was gone. "Thank you for helping me out. I'm sorry I am so sad all the time."

"Don't be sorry. You have a right to be sad for as long as you need." I felt relieved by her words. My emotions were valid, and I didn't have to hide them.

"I think I am going to go to the beach." I sipped my coffee. The warmth was a blanket for my throat. I felt more awake. "My mom loved the beach," I muttered to myself. I wanted to go there for her memory, to honor her in some way.

"That is a great idea!" Sarah acknowledged my thought. Just don't drive yourself.

"I'm not going to drive off a cliff," I stated.

"I know. Just don't go alone. You need company," Sarah insisted.

"Okay, okay; I'll have Dominic come with me." I knew Sarah had to work on the weekend.

"Good." She sat back in her chair. "By the way, you look mighty fine this morning." She smirked.

"Be quiet! I know I look horrible! I have not been able to escape these eye bags!" I laughed and then chugged the rest of my coffee.

* * *

The grains of sand embraced my bare feet while the wind danced through my hair, weaving it into spirals of memories. I replayed memories of Mom and me laughing in Santa Cruz when she was healthy. I thought about that day we are burritos at sunset and her ability to think positive in such a dire state.

It wasn't the California coast; nonetheless, we were at the beach. Newport was an Oregon beach town with windy shores.

Dominic and I set our towels on the sand while the wind fought with us. When we got situated, we sat down and looked at the horizon. I took a deep breath, allowing the salty air into my lungs.

The breeze made it feel chilly, yet the occasional glimpses of sunlight breaking through the clouds offered a warmth that made it more tolerable. I had prepared for the chill with a hoodie and sweats. Underneath, I was wearing my mom's black tankini, a silent tribute to her presence that I couldn't bear to leave behind.

"To the dunes!" My voice cut through the air, igniting a spark of excitement within me. I looked at Dominic to make sure he heard me. With a burst of energy, I sprinted away, and he followed my lead. The adrenaline coursed through my veins as I ran through the wall of wind. I felt free.

Dominic caught up to me quickly, and we reached the summit of the sand dune together. Laughter bubbled up from within me. I felt like a kid again. It was then that Dominic tackled me, his arms wrapping around me and pulling me down to the soft, grainy earth below.

"Hey!" I giggled. Sand was all over me now. I wiped some sand off my chest.

"I couldn't help it," he joked. He gave me a kiss on the cheek.

Out of the corner of my eye, I saw a jagged black rock. I picked it up and felt its rough texture. I held it in my hand, feeling its weight, imagining the stories it held within its rugged surface. It looked ancient.

"This is such a unique rock," I declared. I suddenly had an idea.

"Follow me!" I called out over the howling wind, my heart pounding with anticipation as I dashed toward the crashing waves. Dominic trailed behind me with curiosity as we ventured toward the edge of the sea.

I was close enough to the water without letting my feet get wet. I closed my eyes, summoning every ounce of strength within me.

"This is for my mom!" I shouted into the vast expanse of the ocean as my voice was carried away by the wind. With all my might, I sent the black rock flying through the air, watching as it disappeared into the frothy embrace of the waves below.

"Yes, for Colette!" Dominic shouted in support.

It may have seemed insignificant to an outsider, but to me, it was a symbol of remembrance, a gesture of love and longing. I felt a weight lift off my shoulders, replaced by a sense of peace and closure. Even though my mom was gone, my memories of her were still there. Her spirit was somewhere, hopefully able to appreciate my small gesture.

"Honoring your mom?" Dominic queried.

"Yes," I declared standing up against the wind's restless push. "I know that wasn't much, but it was something I felt like I should do. This is her happy place. This is where I stand." I stood up straighter and put my hands on my hips.

With determination in my voice, I raised my eyes to the sky. "I love you, Mom!" I screamed. My words echoed into the clouds above, carrying my heartfelt message into the heavens. But as quickly as the declaration left my lips, a wave of exhaustion washed over me, leaving me drained. I needed to sit down.

I sat down on the sand, my heart now reminded of how devastating it was to not have a mom anymore.

Dominic sat down on my right facing the direction of the wind to shield me. He put his arm around me and pulled me in tight. I played with my golden necklace, the cross and emblem weaving between my fingers.

"I hope she's happy," I whispered, letting go of the necklace and trying to channel my faith.

"If Heaven is like anything you've told me, then she's happy," Dominic assured me. "I have something for you." He reached into his pocket and pulled out two pieces of heart-shaped dark chocolate.

"Yummy!" I exclaimed, a smile tugging at the corners of my lips. I unwrapped the chocolate and plopped it in my mouth. My taste buds danced, and I felt a hint of pleasure warming my body.

"Wow, this is a perfect day to honor my mom—beach, chocolate, and love." I grinned.

"Did you just say love?" Dominic questioned. The sentiment lingered in the air between us. I hadn't told him I loved him. I wasn't sure I could with my heart being so tangled with grief. *Was it possible to love with a broken heart?*

"How's the chocolate?" I deflected, steering the conversation elsewhere.

"Just like you said, yummy!" He grinned back, his eyes twinkling with affection.

We watched the crashing waves until our toes got cold from the wind. When we turned to leave, tears welled in my eyes, the weight of my loss again, pressing heavily upon me.

"I don't want to go," I admitted, my voice thick with emotion. Dominic spun around to face me.

"We can come back again, Jem." He stooped down and picked up a shell. "Here. A little something to remember the day." I held the quarter size shell in my hand. It was white with vibrant orange stripes on it. The edges were smooth against my fingertips.

"Thanks," I murmured. Tears were still tracing down my cheeks.

I turned toward the sea and let my heart fill with the love of my mom once more. The unintrusive beauty of the ocean was a visual reminder to appreciate the little things. *"Attitude gratitude,"* I whispered to myself.

SEVENTEEN

"How many miles did you run?" my therapist asked in a stern and clear voice. I needed a therapist. I was tired of crying in front of everyone. Little did I know that I would feel anger too

"Just eight miles," I answered timidly in front of the screen. There was no way I was going to see her in person. A Zoom appointment felt more distant.

"How hard did you run?" she asked, her eyes locked on mine.

"Umm, just like a 6:30 pace. . ." I hesitated to answer.

Dr. Mindy's eyes widened in shock, and her gaze looked straight into the video camera directly at me. I could see the look of concern spread across her face. Her attention was focused on me, her shoulder-length bright blonde hair remained stagnant, and her posture didn't move for a solid twenty seconds.

I felt uncomfortable, so I looked away from the camera, hoping that Zoom couldn't catch my discomfort. I waited for what she had to say.

"Jem, you're doing it again," she reminded me softly. "You are self-sabotaging. You have to listen to your body and rest when it needs rest. You are tired and sad from mourning your mom, and you need to give yourself a break."

I shifted in my seat. I had been feeling pain in my left foot because grieving combined with running was creating too much stress on my foot. But I tried to explain my side to Dr. Mindy.

"Dr. Mindy, I *NEED* to run. I *HAVE* to run. It helps me process my emotions." I needed to run or else my thoughts would consume me and tear me apart.

"Jem, you need to rest. There are other ways to cope with your emotions. Draw, read, yell into a pillow, journal, and many more. Running high mileage weeks at full speed along with the weight of grief will be too stressful to your body, and you can get seriously injured. And then you won't even be able to run. Do you really want to be injured in your last season?"

"But . . . ," I stammered defensively. "I will go crazy if I can't run! You can't take that away from me! I already lost my mom! I can't lose running too!" I was almost shouting at the camera.

"Jem, you already told me that you are exhausted every day, and I can even see through the screen that you have bags under your eyes. Deep ones." She took a deep breath. "What do you think your mom would say to you if she was here?" She peered at me with her bright green eyes.

Instantly, anger raged within me. I was furious.

"You can't pull that!" I yelled as heat inflamed my body. "You're trying to make me feel guilty about running too much!" I was so angry that I wanted to hit the cancel button on the screen. I paused for a moment. *What would my mom say? She would tell me to rest. She would hold me in her arms and kiss the top of my head and tell me that everything was going to be okay.*

She would tell me resting would make me stronger. She'd say, "Jem, honey, I see you're exhausted, come sit with me and let's read on the couch." But she wasn't there. She was gone.

"I can do what I want; it doesn't matter anymore!" I yelled. I almost flung my laptop off the table with rage. Mom wasn't here; Dr. Mindy couldn't use that against me.

Dr. Mindy kept quiet.

Almost instantly, my rage turned to sadness, and I wanted to cry. I wanted a hug from my mom. I wanted to read with her on the ugly green couch. I wanted to dance for her and shake my booty, to make her laugh.

Dr. Mindy was right. My mom would want the best for me, to be healthy. I sighed.

"Rest for her," Dr. Mindy said in a quiet tone close to a whisper. "It's okay to do it for her and not for you."

"I'm sorry. I know my mom would tell me to rest, but I don't know how. I don't know what to do. Running is my therapy." A tear started to drift out of my eye socket, but I blinked rapidly to send it back. If one tear came out, a billion more would soon follow.

"This is your therapy, Jem," she said tenderly. She eyed me with compassion. "It's going to be hard to rest, but I believe in you, and I know your mom believed in you. Just try to imagine what she would say if she was with you now and try to channel that. You owe it to her, and you owe it to you."

I nodded through the screen and listened to her advice until time was up. When I was all alone, I stared out the window as the tear that I held back fell down my cheek.

"Mom," I said, "I'm trying." I peered at the pear tree outside.

* * *

Everything that was mentioned in therapy was forgotten, and I laced up my shoes for another eight-mile run. There was no other choice. It was my habit, my ritual.

Seven miles into the run, I felt a snap in my left foot. I stopped to assess it. It had already started to turn pink. I poked the left side of my foot where I felt the snap. It was extremely tender.

I began to run again, and the pain throbbed. I stopped again, this time to stretch it. It was no use. It was injured. I hobbled home in disappointment. I did this to myself.

The sports doctor told me that my foot injury was categorized as a stress response. This is the step just before a stress fracture, which was a minor break. I had to be careful.

I could still compete in the track season, but I would need to strictly use the stationary bike and rest from running. Dr. Mindy's voice rang in my ears. *What would your mom say to you if she was here?* She would say *attitude, gratitude.* And because of that, I decided to be grateful and ride on the stationary bike.

* * *

Now, the pain came in waves. I'd be fine for a day but then the next, there'd be a tsunami.

"I'm not that strong. I can't do this," I cried, bursting into tears. "I miss her so much. You don't know how much she meant to me."

I buried my head into Dominic's chest, drenching his shirt. We were standing in the park, a place we now met regularly. We would walk to the park and then swing on the swings and stay there until I calmed down.

"Something inside me has been ripped out. It's hard to explain. It's all so debilitating." The more I wiped my tears away, the more came.

I let go of him and sat on the swing, looking down at the sand. Dominic said nothing, and he took the swing next to mine. Swinging usually calmed me, but today, it didn't.

I jumped off the swing and started sprinting away.

"Jem! Jem! Stop!" I could hear Dominic behind me. I didn't stop, and I didn't look back. I jogged through the neighborhood and back to my house, my left foot throbbing with each step. When I got there, I slammed the door shut and fell to the floor hyperventilating.

A few minutes later, Dominic joined me on the floor. My breathing had steadied somewhat, and I found myself gazing absently at the ceiling. I felt his fingers brush against mine, then our hands were entwined. He lay there beside me, our fingers in a quiet embrace of unspoken understanding.

"I don't know why I ran," I managed to say, wiping my eyes with my shirt.

"I don't know either. You are still grieving, and sometimes people do crazy stuff when they are in pain." He pulled a strand out of my hair.

"Yeah," I sniffled. Perhaps that's why people do crazy things—because they have pent-up emotions they can't control.

"And you know what?" Dominic interrupted my thoughts. "Your mom is probably smiling down on you from Heaven right now." He smiled at me, and tears rolled down his cheeks. He squeezed my hand.

I felt comforted by him. There was no way I could do this alone.

"I will stay with you as long as you want," he vowed.

I cried some more, and then my eyes went dry; my head hurt, and I needed another hug. Dominic hugged me, rubbed my back, and brought me tissues.

"Shall we have some tea?" Dominic suggested. "And maybe some chocolate too?"

I couldn't remember the last time I ate. Crying masked my hunger.

After sipping tea on the patio, I gradually regained my composure and felt more grounded. Despite the fact that crying sucked, I felt cathartic after.

"I think it's time for me to go pray," I decided.

Dominic and I went our separate ways because I wanted to pray alone. Dr. Mindy agreed, though she wasn't religious, that turning to prayer was healthier than running. I didn't want to abuse running anymore. I needed to be kind to my body. But also, I needed to be kind to my soul. That's where prayer came in.

Instead of wearing my usual attire of gray sweats and a hoodie, I slid into my light blue dress, an outfit to honor my mom. Sky blue was her favorite color.

I snuck out the door by the garage, careful not to be heard by Sarah. I didn't feel like talking. If she saw me, she'd ask me how I was, and I didn't want to lie and say I was good. *How many times can somebody deal with my sadness?* I didn't want to take that chance. No one wants to be around someone who is always sad. Dominic was so selfless to be with me. I didn't even want to be around me.

"Just persevere, Jem." I whispered to myself as I walked toward the church. Luckily, everything in Corvallis was within walking distance. I loved that about the town.

Even though I could pray anywhere, I went back to the chapel. The stained-glass windows brought beauty to the space, which made it easier to pray.

I strolled through the neighborhood, my foot aching just a bit. I passed by a rose bush. I stared at one of the bubblegum pink buds, perfectly symmetrical, and tried to appreciate it as I thought, *it's so pretty that I want to enjoy it forever. Mom would have loved to enjoy this rose. Is she enjoying it too? Can she see it from Heaven? Hey, Mom, can you see it from Heaven?*

I didn't know if my mom could read my mind while she was in Heaven, and I didn't know if she was even watching me right now. I bet she was busy talking to saints. Of course, she was; there were many great saints in Heaven. *Mom, if you're available, I want to show you this pretty rose,* I thought. *I think it's beautiful just like you. I wish I could pick it up for you. I wish I could hug you. I wish I could . . .*

Tears started to form. *Shoot. Not again! I've got to get to the chapel.* I turned my head around to see if anyone else was watching. There was nobody. *Phew.*

I abandoned the rose and swiftly darted away. I made it to the chapel unseen by anyone. I entered, using both hands to pull the heavy doors open.

I kneeled in silence with my mind fixed on the beauty of the gold trimmings around the tabernacle. How nice it was that Jesus was wrapped in gold instead of hanging on the cross. What a journey it was for Jesus to go from nails to glory.

I believed Mom went from earth to Heaven. *Was the journey long? Does Heaven have beautiful gold?*

I felt a hand on my shoulder. I turned around to see that it was Father Max, my favorite priest.

"*Salve,* Jem," he whispered. *Salve* was Latin for hello. Father Max was from Argentina, and he spoke both English and Spanish. His role was to help guide college students to the faith.

He gave me a quick smile and then his face turned serious.

"God does not permit unnecessary suffering," He asserted. I pondered what he had said. *Does he mean that my suffering was necessary? I needed to be sad?* Before I could articulate my thoughts, he continued.

"Remember that Jesus is your strength." He patted me on the back once more and turned around. Before I could say anything, he disappeared down the aisle and was gone.

Okay, Jesus, I prayed. *I could really use some strength. I really have nothing left to give.* I closed my eyes now as if it helped me reach Him.

Suddenly, I felt this intense desire to let go. Something inside me felt weighted, and I needed to release it from my grip. This burden felt as though it was hanging on my heart, choking my ability to love fully. *Lord, I surrender to You. My life is Yours. My burdens are Yours. My sufferings are Yours. My joys are Yours. You can have it all.* I took a big deep breath.

Almost immediately, the weight I felt inside vanished. The heaviness had lifted off my shoulders. The tension melted from my muscles, and my face relaxed. There was an absence of worry.

My knees began shaking. It had been over an hour since I kneeled. I leaned my body back and sat on the pew. I gazed at the tabernacle one last time. *Jesus, I trust in You*, I declared in my heart.

My body stilled, and I could feel my heartbeat in my chest. It was a magical rhythm. It was so magical; I didn't need to do anything to make it beat; it just did. By the power of God, I was alive, and by the power of God, I had peace. *Did I need suffering to remind me of my reliance on faith?*

I needed Jesus most. He was the unchangeable force in my life. I knew that. No matter what, He was here. And He was good.

Leaving the chapel brought a sense of liberation. Surrendering had granted me the freedom to share with Jesus my suffering. Sharing was less hard than holding it myself. I trotted back home, pausing to inhale the scent of the rose bush one last time.

EIGHTEEN

"It's just not fair," Dad shouted over the phone. There was a rising anger in his words. I was uncertain how to respond.

"I know it's not fair, but we're just going to have to trust God," I answered.

"What do you mean?" he stammered. "I prayed for your mom, and she wasn't healed!" His voice was raised, and he sounded even angrier than before. I could feel him pacing around the room, all alone in the house he once shared with Mom.

I imagined he had tears in his eyes, but I couldn't quite tell over the phone. He was hiding it too well.

"God is sad too," I explained. "He didn't want Mom to be in pain or for us to be sad."

"Then why didn't he heal her?!" he yelled. I had to pull the phone back from my ear because his voice was too loud. Frankly, I was scared to respond, but I had to stand up for God.

"I don't know," I said quietly. "But I do know that He loves Mom and loves us all. His love is unconditional. And He's here to take our burdens away." Maybe my dad needed to surrender his burdens in prayer.

Silence followed. Dad was not happy with my answer. He swore under his breath, a new habit he had obtained after Mom's death. I stayed quiet. I didn't know what else to say. Then, I heard the tears.

"I miss her so much." Dad sniffled. "I just miss her so much." I wished I could reach my arm through the phone and pat his back and give him a bear hug. He needed some love. *God, please watch over my dad and love him*, I prayed silently.

"I do too. So much," I agreed, feeling a heaviness in my heart. "We have to have hope," I declared.

After I hung up, I walked to the kitchen to finish the dark chocolate bar Dominic had given me. Frustration had made me hungry. When I got to the kitchen, I found Sarah sitting at the kitchen table.

"Hey, I overheard your conversation." She bent her head low to signal the mood and that she was sorry for overhearing.

"Yeah. It's hard to explain faith." I sat down across from her, grateful for her company.

"Do you know what you can do?" She gazed at me with empathy, her heart beating the same pace as mine.

"I think I know what you're thinking." My eyes locked on hers. Of course, I knew.

"Pray!" we declared at the same time smiling at each other.

"I haven't stopped praying since before it happened. I even said a short prayer during the phone conversation," I disclosed. "It is the only thing that I can do. I can't heal cancer. I can't heal grief. I can't make my family happy. I can't make things right, but God can. He can give meaning to all this. I just don't know what His purpose is." I slumped down in a chair across from Sarah. *What was God's purpose?*

"You may never know God's purpose, but you have to trust that it is all for good." There was a twinkle in her eye that revealed her faith.

"Yes, that's what I tried to explain to my dad." I sighed. "I'm just not very good at it."

"But you must also remember, Jem, praying never goes to waste." She held my light blue rosary in her hand and placed it on the table in front of me. I must have left it downstairs by accident. "You're not one to back down from prayer. Just keep persevering."

"Thanks, Sarah. I really appreciate it." I held the rosary in my hand anticipating the strength it would give me. "Prayer is the strongest weapon," I declared.

"Sure is." She nodded in agreement. "Now would you like to pray the Rosary out by the rose bush?"

* * *

The next day, Dominic stopped by on his way home from work. When I opened the door, I just slumped into his chest. At this point, we both knew that I would be in this position for a while.

I was snug in Dominic's embrace when his phone buzzed. Being nosey I asked, "Who texted you?"

"Uh, it's nothing." He shrugged it off.

"What do you mean it's nothing? Who is it from?" I inquired, sounding irritated.

"It's from my mom. She asked how my day was going."

"Oh," I answered in a deflated tone. That's why he didn't want to share. He didn't want to make me sad. I looked down trying not to think about how I will never receive a text from my mom ever again.

"I think you should tell her you love her. I think she would love to hear it," I suggested. "You can never express 'I love you' enough," I added. I wanted to mention it could be the last opportunity, but that felt too grim. Yet, to me, it was simply realistic.

"Okay, I will," he smiled as he texted her back.

I was honestly proud of myself for reacting that way. It was important that I slowly accept the subjects of moms. Dr. Mindy would be proud.

"What do you want to do tonight?" Dominic asked as he slid his phone into his jean pocket.

"You know I think I am going to go pray. I need some alone time with Jesus." After the conversation with my dad, I just found prayer to be essential, more so than before.

"Again?" His voice sounded agitated. Perhaps I didn't hear him right.

"Yes, again," I answered slowly. "I need Jesus more than ever, and you can never pray enough."

Dominic's facial expression changed. He was angry.

"Why do you think praying works?" he challenged. "You go pray five times a day, and then nothing happens!" His voice was sharp and jagged like a sword sliced in front of me.

"Because it does!" I argued back. I had no evidence off the tip of my tongue. My mind went blank. I was shocked with what he was saying. I thought he believed in prayer. He sounded like my dad. "God is good," I muttered. Surely, He was good. Why couldn't he see that?

"It's like you're obsessed with praying, and you think praying is better than hanging out with me!"

It struck hard. How could he compare those things? Praying was incomparable to anything. It was a spiritual connection. I didn't have that with Dominic; he was just my boyfriend.

Then it made sense. He was jealous that I was spending too much time with Jesus and none with him. I kept decreasing our time together, so I could go pray.

"How can you even say that?!" I felt my cheeks flush and my voice rise. I stepped away from him. I needed some space.

"You dance around and say that Jesus hears you, and He loves you! Well sorry to break it to you, but your mom is dead, and Jesus heard nothing! I know you claim that God is good, but I don't believe you anymore!"

My head was spinning. Why was he saying those things? I thought he was understanding faith, the belief in something good even when it is unseen. And I hated—hated that he brought that up about my mom. How could he? That was my wound, and he just stabbed it with his invisible knife.

There is so much that goes on in the world. He didn't understand about natural evil like diseases and hurricanes or about moral evil, which is the choice we humans make. No, he understood the world as God is in control of everything. We are not God's puppets. We have free will. We can't blame God.

I was crying now, more upset than sad. I couldn't be with someone who didn't believe and support my prayer life. If there was no Jesus, there was no Heaven, no hope. What was the point of life then? It would be pointless. I couldn't fathom how someone could live like that.

I couldn't believe Dominic's words. There was no way I could get past them now. It was over. Our relationship, our bond was over. My thoughts were fuzzy, and I didn't realize Dominic was staring at me, waiting for me to say something.

"It's over," I declared firmly. "We're done. I can't be with someone who doesn't love Jesus."

When Dominic left, I wept uncontrollably for the rest of the evening. He was gone, and with him, our relationship. If he didn't know Jesus, I wouldn't know how to be with him. Yet, even in his absence, I missed him deeply. Now, there were two people I loved who had lost their faith. I cried myself to sleep.

NINETEEN

O nce more, the familiar scent enveloped me—the blossoming flowers in a tie-dye of colors, the fresh dew under the morning sun. As I savored my habitual routine of admiring the flowers, I couldn't help but wonder again if my mom, too, was taking joy in their beauty.

Spring had an aroma of promise. I felt as though God was promising me that good things were going to happen. My eyes were peeled for it.

With Dominic out of my life, I mourned for him. And when I mourned for him, I longed for comfort from my mom, in which I mourned even more. It was a new ending cycle of doom.

But God was good, and I firmly believed it. I had to keep moving forward. I had to have hope because hope doesn't disappoint.

I was making enough progress in school that I could participate in class and not feel the invisible wall of isolation around me. Even training was going better, and I was able to go to practice twice a week and run with the team without crying halfway through. I still rode the stationary bike, following Dr. Mindy's orders and not running too much.

It was almost the end of the track season. I hadn't run a single race. But today, Coach Lewis surprised me.

"You're going to the track championships. The 3k Steeplechase," Coach Lewis confirmed. "I want you there." He patted my back. Wide-eyed and completely shocked, I answered the only way I could.

"Okay!" My words mixed with confusion and excitement. Although I wasn't in perfect shape, I was still fast. Although my foot wasn't healed, I could run on it. But on top of it all, I felt honored to be chosen.

The appreciation didn't last long because nerves came creeping in. I didn't know what to expect. Sure, I was back to a semi-normal training schedule, but I was still mentally unengaged, with grief clouding my mind at unexpected times. I was really taking a risk by competing.

"Jem, we just lost our mom. The fact that you are still going to compete is amazing," Mara reassured me over the phone. "You don't have to prove anything. Toeing the line is the biggest success." She was always so supportive of me.

Mara had me reenergized with purpose. Her pep talks could always lift my spirits. She was right. Months ago, my body could barely function. I had a stress response, and I was getting yelled at in therapy. Now, I was making progress, feeling sixty-five percent of my normal compared to the five percent that I had previously felt.

"By the way, you should know that we're all coming," Mara noted.

"What do you mean by 'we'?" I didn't feel like anyone was going anywhere. The track meet was in LA, miles away from San Jose and Seattle.

"Dad, Micah, and I. Of course, we are going to watch you in your last track meet ever!" She sounded proud, and my face lit up.

"Really?!" I exclaimed. I pumped my fist into the air even though she couldn't see it. "Wait, what if I run really slow? I'm not in the best shape." My worries held onto my words.

"Like I said. We don't care how you do. After all that we've been through, it's already a win."

"Thanks, Mara!" I beamed, feeling grateful that I was supported and happy that I got one last chance to compete.

"Oh, and I got a tattoo," she added.

"What?" I was confused. It felt out of the blue.

"You know how *Colette* means people of victory in French? Well, I got it written on my arm in her handwriting." Everything about that tattoo sounded amazing. I couldn't wait to see it.

"Send me a pic, pronto!" I insisted. "You know, Mom really was victorious, even in her last days, she claimed victory by choosing to see the good."

"She really was. That's why I needed to get this tattoo, to remind me of her victorious spirit. I will show you it in person. I got to go now; I love you!"

"I love you too, sis!" I hung up the phone and stared at the screen. I loved my sister. I loved my family.

Things were going to be okay.

* * *

NINETEEN

Sweat dripped from my forehead and into my eyes. I awoke from a nightmare; I had tried to tell my mom I loved her one more time, but she had already passed away. The void in my heart throbbed.

I stepped out of the hotel bed and onto the jaded carpet. It was race day, and I was unmotivated and exhausted. I peered at myself in the bathroom mirror and saw that my eye bags were thick. *Did I even sleep?*

I ran my fingers through my hair and tied it up in a ponytail. Whether I wanted it or not, race day was here. *Jesus, I trust in You,* I prayed, hoping He heard me.

The journey to the track was accompanied by a commotion of honks and beeps. Los Angeles sprawled in chaotic energy. Observing the surroundings during the drive affirmed what I'd been told—LA truly embodied the essence of a concrete jungle. I could count on one hand how many trees there were. So far, I had counted three.

When it got close to race time, I slipped on my bright orange Nike shoes and clicked through Spotify for a song to ease my nerves. I played "For the Good" by Riley Clemmons. The song spoke about trusting God on the broken road and the promise that He will work things out for the good. It was that message that I needed to hear most. *Hope does not disappoint.* I had to remind myself of that.

I headed to the warm-up area, which was a set of two turf fields. Two of my teammates were joining me in the Steeplechase race. We were the brave ones to run seven and a half laps around the track and go against the dreaded water jump.

Gianna and Katherine ripped off their sweats and started their stretches. I trudged along behind them, my body feeling heavier than normal. They were in good spirits, which made me feel a little bit worse.

The nightmare had triggered a physical tightness in my limbs. My legs and hips felt sore, and I wanted to lie in bed. I scanned around me. There were so many talented athletes running all around. I felt like a fraud.

"Ready to do our warm-up jog?" Gianna happily asked. Her passion for competing brought her endless energy. I knew she was ready for this race. I, however, was not. I was not mentally or physically ready, but I had to try.

"Yeah, sure." Although I didn't want to move, I knew that I had to.

"Let's get off this turf and run around campus," Katherine suggested. I stripped off my sweatpants and followed their lead. We took off through the campus. The University of California had beautiful architecture, but foliage was nonexistent.

A minute into the run, both my teammates were already five steps ahead of me. The defeat in my mind grew bigger. *How am I going to do this?*

I let them continue going, and I slowed down a little. Nerves and heat were punching me from all angles. It was like I was in a boxing match with no protection. I was out of shape and scared.

I started to dread the race instead of feeling eagerness to compete. I had fought through the grief of my mom while still managing to run. Though I had not been the nicest to my body and my foot was still injured, I was here. I put in the work, and

I did my best in my circumstance. However, I felt embarrassed. I used to be so fast; now, I was just average.

Suddenly, I sensed a motion from my right eye, and I turned my head to see what it was. There, floating in front of me was a hummingbird. I couldn't believe it.

The hummingbird danced in front of me, peaceful as ever. It was glowing with many colors. I blinked to make sure it was real. The bird fluttered in front of me as if it was trying to say hello. It felt familiar.

That was when I knew. The hummingbird was for me.

Tears spilled out of my eyes, and my heart felt a sensation of abundant love inside. Instantly, I thought of the joy my mom had when she saw the hummingbird months ago.

I blinked hard, but the tears kept coming. This felt too personal. *Could it be?* Immediately I felt as though my mom's voice was saying, "Remember the small joys." I said it out loud to confirm as if the hummingbird could understand me.

Then, the beautiful bird flew away into the city streets before me. There were no flowers and no trees. There was no wildlife and no water. There was just one hummingbird alone, but completely and purposely for me.

My heart pumped with a warm sensation that I only received in my deepest prayer moments. God had revealed a hummingbird just for me. There was no doubt.

Remember the small joys.

I was competing. I had made it to my last track meet. I had used running to help me grieve. I was surrounded by teammates I loved and my amazing family. And now I was sure that my mom was watching too, from Heaven.

I also saw a hummingbird, a true sign of God's love.

My legs began moving faster, an energy source from joy. My mom was in Heaven, and God was good. It was going to be okay. Today wasn't going to be about winning for me; it was going to be about focusing on the small things. The joys were abundant; I just needed to become aware.

Fifteen minutes later, I am on the starting line. It was just about seven thirty, and I could see the colors of the sun at its early setting. The tangerine and magenta rays were vivid. I stood there staring at it, smiling while the other runners did their last-minute warm-up routines.

I turned to a girl next to me who was a stranger from another team.

"Hey, look at the sunset! It's beautiful!" I marveled. I stood there, gazing at it, taking it all in. The girl ignored me and turned away. I had no feelings toward her. I just stared back at the sunset, admiring its beauty and being filled with hope. Tonight was a beautiful day for a race, and there was nothing that could stop me from enjoying it.

When the gun went off, I ran my hardest to get into the top group. I got up to fifth in the midst of twenty girls. I felt strong with my new joyful energy. After mile one, my body started to ache, and I had to slow down, but it wasn't going to steal my joy. I glanced up at the sunset again and appreciated the warm colors.

Each lap, I felt more tired. In addition, my foot started throbbing. My fifth place slipped away from me. I wasn't going to call defeat.

As girls passed me, I decided to cheer for them. I called "good job" to them, with a smile. I was proud of them because they were doing great, and so was I. This was something I didn't think was possible.

When I fell through the finish, body fatigued and warped, I cried. I ran that race with joy, with the same mindset as my mom. Just like when she found joy in the hummingbird in her boney and limited body, I too found joy during a hard race and dealing with my body's incapabilities.

It didn't matter that my foot was hurt, and I didn't score. Mom had taught me that if good things get taken away from you, there is still good. There is always good. Sometimes, you just have to search harder for it.

Coach Lewis, Gianna, and Katherine huddled around me.

"Is everything okay?" They saw the tears clutching to my face and my unusual finish of tenth place. I smiled to let them know I was fine.

"I'm good. I'm just glad my mom was able to watch me." I gazed up at the sky indicating that she was observing me from above. Gianna started tearing up, and she threw her arms around me.

"She saw everything, and you did great!" She celebrated. I knew that my greatness fell short physically but not spiritually. My heart was on fire with love and gratitude. I had felt my mom through that hummingbird. She had reassured me of the good in the world. The greatness inside of me was recreating the true meaning of life itself, to find the small joys.

I hustled over to the stands where I met up with Mara, Micah, and Dad. They each gave me a hug and a word of affirmation.

"Way to go, Champ!" Dad patted me on the back, perfectly proud.

"You held that girl off in the end," Micah commended. I had no clue what he was talking about. I had barely focused on the race itself.

"Mom would be proud," Mara confirmed. "And as your sister, I am proud too!" She gave me a shoulder squeeze.

"That was the first race," I confessed, my voice trembling with newfound clarity, "that I wasn't weighed down by my expectations. I finally ran for the sheer love of it, proud to be a part of it, and it was liberating."

The announcer's voice from the meet faded into the background as I stood there, feeling truly victorious for the first time in a long while. For in that pivotal moment, I didn't just win a race; I reclaimed my passion and rediscovered the joy that had been buried beneath layers of grief and expectation. I had won the race because I had found joy again.

It wasn't until I had a moment alone to thank God for all that He had shown me.

I still don't know Your plan but thank You for that hummingbird, I whispered in my heart, quietly with praise.

* * *

When I got back to Oregon, I immediately wrote everything down in my journal. There was no way I could ever forget that moment. The hummingbird and the weight of certainty I had were no coincidence. In terms that I could describe, it was a Godsidence.

Evidently enough, I had forgotten that I told my mom to write me a letter for graduation. It was weeks away, but to me it seemed like tomorrow, so I went over to my sock drawer where I had hidden it.

I stared at the brown envelope, a color distinct from all the rest, just like Mom was to me. I stopped. *Should I rip it open or wait?* I ripped it open.

My mom had plastered a real photo of a picture of a beautiful sunset that she had taken. It was just as salmon-colored as the one I witnessed at the track meet. *A Godsidence.*

I was crying before I even read the words on the paper. Just seeing her handwriting drove me to tears. How elegant was her cursive. I could barely read through my tears, but one line stood out to me over all the rest:

> *Thank you for giving me reasons to look at the world differently and to accept all the love from God and others to live my best life.*

My heart softened completely. I was overwhelmed with warmth, love, and gratitude. While my mom believed that I was supporting her through her battle with cancer, it was actually her who helped me. She reminded me of life's small joys. In the end, we supported each other through this journey.

"How was the track meet?" Sarah asked, her eyes bright with curiosity.

"There was a Godsidence!" I exclaimed on my tippy toes.

"What's a Godsidence?" she asked, tilting her head to show her confusion.

"It's when things happen perfectly while certainly knowing that God was in control of it all." I flashed a big smile her way. "And you know what's for sure." I was confident about this one. "I don't know God's plan, but I know that He is good. And if

He is good, then everything will end up good. I know it." *Hope does not disappoint.*

A couple days later, I got a call from Ariana. I hadn't seen her in a while. She probably forgot that I had quit lifeguarding.

"Hello?" I answered.

"Hey! It's me, Ariana. I know this is random, but can we meet? I have something that I really want to give you." Her tone was cheerful but also persistent. "Can you meet me at the lifeguard station in thirty minutes?" It was four thirty. Her shift must end at five.

"Sure, yeah. I'll bike over soon." We hung up, and I couldn't help but question what she had for me. It sounded like a gift, but I wasn't too sure. It was probably goggles that I had left there.

When I entered the gym, I walked to the lifeguard station. I slumped into the empty seat to wait for her release. I saw her out on the pool deck bobbing her head to the beat of the music.

Fumbling with the height of my chair in ratio with the table, I was resetting adjustments, so I could lean my head down without an awkward round in my back. While I was doing so, Ariana popped into the office.

She was upbeat and peppy as usual. When she saw me, her eyes lit up even brighter, which made us both break out into large smiles. Ariana's Latino facial structures and big brown eyes mixed well with her cheery disposition and big heart. I always felt so good when she was near.

"Hey, girl, I am so glad you came! I have something for you!" She tossed her backpack on the table and her fingers thumbed through a couple binders and folders until she pulled out a piece of paper. She held it in her chest as if it was a baby.

"One of my hobbies is painting," she admitted. "And I was painting this picture, and I immediately thought of you. There was a strange feeling inside me, and I just knew I had to give it to you." Her eyes widened. She was talking fast and enthusiastically, which got me really excited for what she had created. "I don't know why, but I really want you to have it!"

Anticipation rising, she turned the paper over. With a mix of oranges, yellows, and reds, it was a beautiful picture of a hummingbird with emerald leaves in the background.

I gasped and stared. I blinked my eyes rapidly, so no tears came out.

"This is incredible," I announced. "Truly incredible!" I studied the painting more, getting my nose inches away from the canvas paper. I turned back to Ariana.

"Thank you so much," was all I could muster out of my mouth.

I gave Ariana a monster hug. I glanced back at the artwork in my hands and couldn't believe my eyes. My thoughts raced. Of all the animals Ariana could paint, she painted a hummingbird. There was no way that was a coincidence. Another Godsidence. There was no way. Three signs, three instances, and three reasons to claim that God is good.

I wasn't exactly sure what he was trying to say in this picture; maybe He was saying, *"Your mom's alright, Jem,"* or perhaps, *"Focus on the small joys."* But I knew for sure that he was saying, *"I love you"* in His own beautiful and perfect way. A teardrop moistened my grateful smile.

I was filled with peace.

TWENTY

On the third anniversary of my mom's death, it takes me roughly ten minutes to cry for her after I wake. I wipe my eyes, and I say a prayer for her and her happiness in Heaven.

I want her to be happy. I knew she was happy. She gave me clarity on that.

I slid my crazy fuzzy slippers on, the ones that look like bunnies were attached to my feet and I didn't dare to change out of my sweatpants. If there was any day to wear sweats, it was this day. One automatically gets extended grace for dealing with death.

On the walk to the chapel, I took note of the nature around me, simply beautiful as it was. Before entering the chapel Father Max pulls me aside.

"What's your mom's name again?" he asked in his vestments.

"Colette." Her name gracefully rolled off my tongue.

"Many prayers to her today in this Mass," he said as he smiled and nodded at me. I smiled back with a full heart, feeling grateful that, on this day, I was exactly where I wanted to be—about to celebrate the Mass with my favorite priest and Jesus Christ.

After the service, I headed back to my house to mourn alone. On my third step forward, Father Max stops me.

"Jem," he called. I turned to him intently. "There's a hummingbird that comes by my window every now and then and when I see it, I say a prayer for your mom."

About the Author

JJ Carlson is an up-and-coming author from Portola Valley, California, where she resides with her husband. A former track and field and cross-country athlete at Oregon State University, JJ's passion for sports and competition shaped her disciplined and goal-oriented approach to life. She holds both undergraduate and master's degrees in communication and sociology, fields that have deepened her understanding of people, culture, and the power of storytelling.

When she's not immersed in writing, JJ enjoys spending time outdoors, particularly on trail runs, where she finds inspiration. She is also an active member of her local parish, where she participates in community events and contributes to the life of her church.

JJ's writing is deeply influenced by her strong faith, which is a guiding force in her life. Her connection to her belief system infuses her work, bringing a sense of purpose and meaning to her stories. As she continues to grow as a writer, JJ's commitment to both her craft and her faith shapes her unique voice and vision, promising a bright future in the literary world.

www.ingramcontent.com/pod-product-compliance
Lightning Source LLC
Chambersburg PA
CBHW062216080426
42734CD00010D/1908